Shepherds and Lovers

A Guide to Spiritual Leadership and Christian Ministry

by Brian P. Hall

*Dedicated to Ward McCabe,
Elliott Sorge, Frank and Diane Snow*

Paulist Press
Ramsey, N.J.

Other Books
By Brian P. Hall

Hall, Brian P. *Value Clarification as Learning Process: A Sourcebook.* (Guide for Pastoral Counselors.) Paulist Press, New York, 1973.

Hall, Brian P. *Value Clarification as Learning Process: A Guidebook.* (Book of strategies.) Paulist Press, New York, 1973.

Hall, Brian P. and Smith, Maury. *Value Clarification as Learning Process: Handbook for Clergy and Christian Educators.* Paulist Press, New York, 1973.

Hall, Brian P. *The Development of Consciousness: A Confluent Theory of Values.* Paulist Press, New York, 1976.

Hall, Brian P. *Developing Leadership by Stages: A Value-Based Approach to Executive Managment.* Manohar Publications, London and New Delhi, 1979.

Hall, Brian P. and Osburn, Joseph. *Nog's Vision.* Paulist Press, New York, 1976.

Hall, Brian P. *The Wizard of Maldoone.* Paulist Press, New York, 1976.

Hall, Brian P. *The Personal Discernment Inventory.* Paulist Press, New York, 1980.

Hall, Brian P.; Tonna, Benjamin. *God's Plans for Us: A Practical Strategy for Discernment of Spirits.* Paulist Press, New York, 1980.

Hall, Brian P.; Thompson, H. *Leadership through Values: An Approach to Personal and Organizational Development.* Paulist Press, New York, 1980.

Designed and Illustrated by Gloria Claudia Ortíz

Library of Congress
Catalog Card Number: 81-84352

ISBN: 0-8091-2425-4

Published by **Paulist Press**
545 Island Road, Ramsey, N.J. 07446

Printed and bound in the
United States of America

Contents

1. Introduction: The Call to Ministry

"The world exists for the realization in time of God's eternal purposes. Some of these are bound up with individual lives, for God intended each one of us to do and to be something."
(W. R. Inge. *Personal Religion and the Life of Devotion,* 1924, p. 60)

"If we had before us those who have thus been a blessing to us, and could tell them how it came about, they would be amazed to learn what passed over from their lives to ours."
(Albert Schweitzer. *Memories of Childhood and Youth,* 1925, p. 90)

Introduction

This is a book about Shepherds and Lovers. A Shepherd is my analogy for a healthy or spiritual leader and a Lover is the primary sign of Christian ministry. We live in a world that constantly demands us to discern between choices that will lead to either good or evil. Daily we must struggle with decisions that will make us either signs of resurrection or signs of destruction and pain. This is no easy task. To succeed, "to come out on top," we need greater consciousness, more skills, and personal support systems that will enable us to make critical decisions with confidence. Our choices can often lead us to oppose the very institutions that appear to support our day-to-day existence. I have intended this book as a manual for those who strive to be both Shepherds and Lovers.

Two topics we will discuss extensively are ministry and leadership. As Christians, each of us is called to a ministry. Ministry with a small 'm' is the development and exercise of the gifts unique to each of us. Ministry with a capital 'M' refers to the profession of Minister or Priest, a leader in the institutional church. I only wish to note this here as a technical distinction in common usage.

Leadership, because it presumes not only gifts but influence over others, is distinct from ministry. It is a complex issue and developmental in nature, an aspect that I established earlier in a book called *Leadership Through Values*. The point to emphasize here is that although leadership connotes influence over others, we usually think of it as significant influence over others. A parent exercises a very important leadership role in the family. However, the word Leadership in this little book will refer to a person who has a functional role as a leader in an institution or in society, whether a priest or bishop, a banker or the director of a small company. There are, of course, good and bad leaders, leaders with immense power but little lasting influence and leaders with little power but great lasting influence. A Minister with a capital 'M' may therefore be a good or poor leader.

In this context, the leader is a representative of an institution, big or small. The bishop has his diocese, the bank executive his or her bank. The leader, however, is also a person with his or her own values, gifts, and ministry (with a small 'm'). Every leader must struggle with the problem of how to satisfy the institution's needs without compromising his or her own values and gifts. This is an age-old problem. David slew Goliath successfully but did not confront his real problem until he had to lead Israel and remain uncorrupted.

A leader cannot exist without a follower. The two are inextricably bound together, one influencing the other for their mutual growth or destruction. Even Jesus had to contend with Judas. The leader is caught between the Institution and the persons who make up that Institution, illustrated in the diagram below.

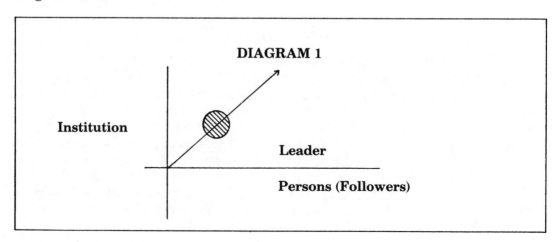

DIAGRAM 1

Institution

Leader

Persons (Followers)

The leader who leads in such a way that the lives of his followers and his own life are enhanced spiritually is a special kind of leader, one we call the Shepherd Lover. An important note to make is that though some have a call to lead, every committed Christian has a ministry, and we all have the potential to minister. A bank manager, for example, is an "ad-ministrator" which means that he or she ministers to someone. Leaders everywhere have varying degrees of power; we cannot all be presidents of a bank or bishops of a diocese. All of us, however, no matter what our role, have the potential to minister though we may not have the skills to do so. The best leaders I know are certain of who they are, what they have to offer, and what they ought not to be doing. In other words, they recognize their gifts, their calling and their ministry.

All Christians have been called to ministry, and our faith tells us that God has given us the gifts to make it possible. Saint Paul described it with the words, "There are different gifts but the same Spirit; there are different ministries but the same Lord; there are different works but the same God who accomplishes all of them in everyone." (New American Bible. 1 Cor. 12:4–6.) We are not called to be leaders and then exercise our ministry; rather, it is just the opposite. We are called first to recognize our gifts. There are many ways to exercise our gifts and talents. Discerning how, in the most effective way possible, is precisely what it means to develop our own unique ministry.

Leadership and Ministry

The essence of leadership is that it involves working within an institution. For a parent, the institution is the family. For a bishop, it is the diocese, or various agencies in the diocese, and for a banker, it is the local bank. Institutions are the backbone of our civilization, providing us with the basic necessities of daily living and giving us the opportunity to become civil or civil-ized. At the most basic level, my job gives me the opportunity to provide food, warmth, and shelter for my family. Institutions offer the possibility of education and growth. At a higher level, my work as vocation gives meaning and direction to my life. Because institutions are more rigid than persons, however, we find ourselves caught between our own needs and institutional demands.

There are good and bad institutions just as there are good and bad leaders and not all leaders are shepherds. This brings me to my first major hypothesis: *The phenomena of evil are experienced by each of us as an institutional or system pressure.* Though we may believe it to be pressure from an individual, what we actually experience is the power of the system against us. Satan does not waste his time with individuals unless he can effect change in a larger whole. Evil infiltrates institutions first and then individuals, acting as a powerful and coercive force that converts shepherds into tryants possessed by its energy. The church, the most sacred of institutions, has often been its prime target.

Because we are all called to lead in some capacity, we are inevitably faced with a decision between persons and institutions, between the forces of good and evil. This book for Shepherd Leaders, by addressing this eternal struggle, is a service manual for successful maintenance and growth for yourself and those you are called to love.

System Overview 1

I stated in my first hypothesis that evil is experienced by individuals as institutional pressure. My second hypothesis is as follows: *In order to give spiritually (to love) as a shepherd leader you must successfully address the needs of your system such that the spiritual growth of each person in that system is potentially enhanced.* I use the words "potentially enhanced" because the job of the shepherd is to provide the conditions and opportunities for growth. Whether or not a person grows is up to the individual. Another diagram will illustrate this further.

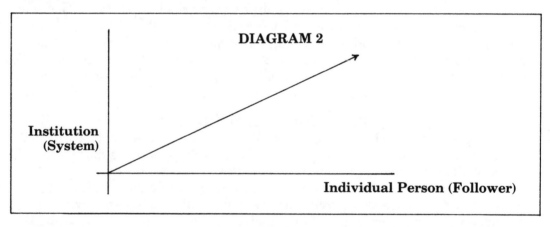

The graph shows that each of us is caught between what our primary experience of institution demands of us and what individuals want from us. Let us suppose that I am the head nurse in a local hospital and hospital policy (Institutional Vector) requires that any staff person who is late more than three times in one month must be fired. We assume this is a reasonable rule because the hospital has lost money three months in a row. However, as head nurse, I have a friend with a family problem who has been late to work three times in the last three weeks. She has already confided to me that her teenage daughter was in a car accident and needs limited home care for three more weeks. In addition, her husband is on an overseas assignment with the army for another six weeks. I am caught between the vectors on our graph, between hospital rules which say that my friend must be fired or at least suspended, and my concern for my friend who needs any help I can give her.

Consider also the friend. Confronted with the hospital rules by the head nurse and told she must not be late again, she finds herself also caught between institution and her daughter's needs. On our diagram this situation would appear as follows:

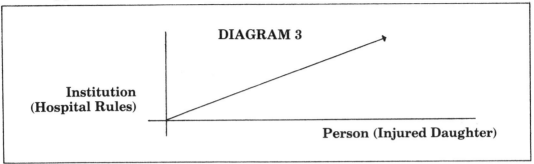

DIAGRAM 3

Institution
(Hospital Rules)

Person (Injured Daughter)

If she adheres to the hospital rules, the friend may be less than what she feels a mother should be to her daughter. Either way she feels guilty. She is caught between institutional and individual needs. Her predicament, however, is even more complicated because she is actually trapped between two institutions, the hospital and her family. This can be illustrated graphically:

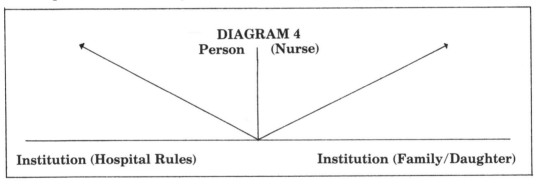

DIAGRAM 4
Person   (Nurse)

Institution (Hospital Rules)   Institution (Family/Daughter)

The friend is caught between persons and institution in two settings simultaneously, a common bind we all experience daily. Much of our guilt and difficulty is not simply personal, but the consequence of the fact that we are "Persons as Systems," a basic reality of everyday life and the struggle to become shepherds. When we ask what she should do in such a situation, we are posing a "ministry" question. The problem is ascertaining her precise ministry in this situation. What choices should she make so that all persons involved would have maximum opportunity for spiritual growth?

This is the primary question not only for the head nurse, but for each of us. To maximize our own spiritual growth as shepherds, we must each spend sufficient time mediating between the needs of institutions and individuals. The pressure, though different in specific circumstances, is nevertheless very real. In 15 years of consultation and spiritual direction to leaders at all levels of institutions, this has been the most crucial issue and one that individual psychotherapy and spiritual direction have failed to address.

A bishop, religious superior, or priest often feels the tension between personal needs for spiritual growth and the demands of church or community. A pastor may say, "I have so many emergencies to deal with, I never seem to have time for myself." An industrial executive says, "We will fall too far behind if I do not attend the meeting on Saturday. I just cannot let someone else go in my place. The family will have to understand." A mother says, "We both work so hard we never seem to be home when the whole family is there together."

What sense can we make of this? We must realize first that institutions are necessary for exceptional individual spiritual growth to occur. We need to develop as persons but we are never persons in isolation. A person is an *individual as System,* a reality that has always been at the heart of the Gospel message: the Christian is not a person in isolation but a part of an enduring community of salvation. Each of us grows in relationship to our primary system of support and nurturance.

Leadership as Servant Ministry

A leader, as we have noted, has influence over the lives of others as well as over his or her own. Though leadership as such could be positive or negative, the understanding that each of us is called to a ministry means that we try to use our influence to enhance the positive spiritual growth of those we encounter. Implied is the need to become aware of the gifts we have to offer and to develop and nurture those gifts in life-giving ways. Having gifts and knowing what they are is not enough, for we must also nurture them by improving our skills and actualize them in practice. As Robert Greenleaf says, "The demonic of this world are those leaders who refuse to lead."

Ironically, a leader must also be a good follower, a paradox called Servant Leadership. Robert Greenleaf describes it as follows:

> The idea of the Servant Leader came out of reading Hermann Hesse's *Journey to the East.* In this story we see a band of men on a mythical journey, probably also Hesse's own journey. The central figure of the story is Leo who accompanies the party as the servant who does menial chores, but who also sustains them with his spirit and his song. He is a person of extraordinary presence. All goes well until Leo disappears. Then the group falls into disarray and the journey is abandoned. They cannot make it without the servant Leo. The Narrator, one of the party, after some years of wandering, finds Leo and is taken into the Order that had sponsored the journey. There he discovers that Leo, whom he had known first as servant, was in fact titular head of the Order, its guiding spirit, a great and noble leader.
> (Robert Greenleaf, *The Servant Leader,* p. 7)

Christian leadership always involves ministry. As ministers, we are called to be servants, servant leaders whose primary job is to follow and allow others to love as did brother Leo.

Jesus of Nazareth, in establishing the community which later became the institution we call Church, was a servant to men, so much so that he was crucified in the process. With the twelve apostles representing the twelve tribes of the older order, Jesus founded an institution that was the new Israel. This new institutional form was meant to serve as his Sermon on the Mount illustrates:

> When he saw the crowds he went up on the mountainside.
> After he had sat down his disciples gathered around him, and he began to teach them:
> 'How blest are the poor in spirit: the reign of God is theirs.
> Blest too are the sorrowing: they shall be consoled.
> Blest are the lowly: they shall inherit the land.
> Blest are they who hunger and thirst for holiness:
> they shall have their fill.
> Blest are they who show mercy: mercy shall be theirs.
> Blest are the single hearted for they shall see God.
> Blest are the peacemakers: they shall be called sons of God.
> Blest are those persecuted for holiness' sake: the reign of God is theirs.
> Blest are you when they insult you and persecute you and utter every kind of slander against you because of me.
> Be glad and rejoice, for your reward is great in heaven: they persecuted the prophets before you in the very same way.'
> (*New American Bible,* Matt. 5:1–12.)

Our Lord's life is the ultimate example of the possible tension between the creative development of an institution and the call to the Shepherd Leader to minister to individuals in need. This tension, in the last analysis, was his cross.

Each of us is called to shepherd as Jesus did. Ministry is the act of integrating institution and the person so that each is spiritually enhanced for the improvement of society. Another diagram will illustrate further.

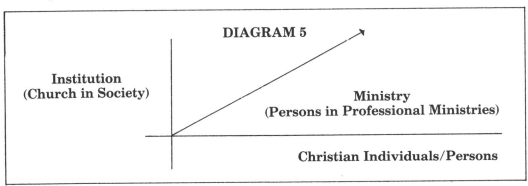

DIAGRAM 5

Institution
(Church in Society)

Ministry
(Persons in Professional Ministries)

Christian Individuals/Persons

Those in professional Ministry, whether bishops, pastors, religious, or any person working in the local congregation such as a hospice worker or pastoral counselor, are engaged in the ministry of enhancing individual spiritual growth and development of the congregation as a whole, two mutually interdependent goals. Sunday liturgy and the management of the church's daily work should interdependently support the growth of persons in community, a goal we strive for, but do not often attain.

This is the beginning of our ministry as Christians: whether we act as leaders or followers, we attempt to humanize our institutions both at home in the family and at work. With this accomplished, we are one step closer to our ultimate vocation to bring about what I call the great "connection" between two systems: the presence of God (the heavenly realm) and life as we experience it on the planet earth (the earthly realm). Illustrated in our graph below is this *evangelical dimension* of ministry:

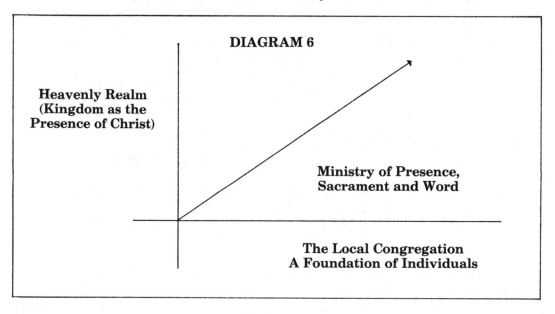

DIAGRAM 6

Heavenly Realm (Kingdom as the Presence of Christ)

Ministry of Presence, Sacrament and Word

The Local Congregation A Foundation of Individuals

Conclusions: Leading and Ministering

In speaking of a person as a leader, we usually refer to an elected or appointed position of power within an institution. The leader has functional power and influence over other people's lives. In the institution of the Church, this position of leadership has come to be known as the Ministry which Hans Kung calls the Ministry Leadership of the Church.

A distinction must be made between Ministry Leadership and Shepherd Leadership, a difference of quality as well as function. There are many Christian leaders who are not Ministers (bishops, priests, or deacons), but need to develop their ministry as shepherds within their respective institutions. These leaders are an integral part of the Church's mission.

Each of us is born with certain gifts and has a unique ministry that needs to be called forth, specified, and developed. We are all called to our own ministries, which for some are positions of leadership. We are not all meant to be leaders; most are summoned to be followers and specialists. Ideally, the leader is chosen because of his or her own talents and the amount of respect he or she holds in the community of follower specialists. In reality it does not often work out that way. Ministry and leadership should coincide in the Christian who becomes what we have named the Shepherd Lover. How this occurs or is threatened is the purpose of this book.

The Shepherd Lover is the link between the followers and the leader: he or she sees the follower as a fellow member of a "We" community in which the leader is a consequence of follower support and the follower is in part the consequence of the leader's ability to structure the institution in such a way that the spiritual life of each individual is enhanced and encouraged. This would be true whether the leader were a bishop or a Silicon Valley executive. How this encouragement is possible is the subject of the next three chapters.

2. The Self: Conversion Consciousness

The real is not veiled from you.
Rather, it is you who are veiled from seeing It;
for, were anything to veil It,
then that which veils It would cover It.
But if there were a covering to It,
then that would be a limitation to Its Being;
Every limitation to anything has power over It.
"And He is the Omnipotent, above His servants."

Ibn 'Ata'illah,
The Bezels of Wisdom, 3,33

Introduction

The human being is the only animal on planet earth that strives throughout its existence for the good in self-defeating ways. Since the beginning of time the human spirit has pursued truth and justice yet the poor are forever oppressed. Since the dawn of consciousness, works of art have praised the creative side within each of us yet we continually misuse the created order. Literature throughout the ages is proof of the great love between men and women expressed both in poetry and song yet there is as much alienation among people today as there was 2000 years ago. Why?

The clear difference between humans and other animals is that we possess and are possessed by consciousness. The early philosophers thought of this as the rational side of being human. Reason, the greatest asset of humanity, makes us, as the psalmist has said, a little less than the angels and a little more than the animals. Unlike animals, we have the ability to be conscious of two things at the same time. While considering and responding to another person or situation, we are able to weigh our own thoughts, feelings, and ideas and put the two events together to make a third response or conclusion. We can drive a car and carry on a conversation, or watch television at the same time that we are studying.

An animal does not possess the same capacity: it sees or hears an event and responds. A dog may dream but it cannot reflect, as far as we know, on that dream; it can only respond as if it were an external event.

The great consciousness event in history was the emergence of the human imagination. We humans not only can reflect on our dreams and fantasies, but we can project our fantasies on to others and feel, to some extent, what they feel. This is empathy, the primary ingredient of loving. What makes this imagination so wonderful is that it, like God the Father in the book of Genesis, can create something out of nothing, an action called "synergy." Two people may have two apparently unrelated ideas when suddenly from the imagination of one springs a new and hitherto unthought-of idea that will change the course of history.

For example, perhaps while wandering through a desert looking for water, someone pondered the idea, "If only I had wings and could fly as fast as the birds in the sky, I could be out of the desert before nightfall." He meets a friend with whom he shares his idea and she imagines, "If only we could run free like the wild horse." Suddenly one of them has an incredible insight: suppose the horse could be tamed and we could ride upon its back. Such an idea, far from new to us, changed the entire course of human history. For nearly 3000 years the horse was the only form of rapid transit over land for the majority of the human race. Commerce, communications, and the movement of whole populations depended on it. Language, mathematics, and the entire history of science abounds with these products of the human reflective consciousness.

As we are only too aware, however, with the good news came the bad, the dark side of human history with its wars, oppression, and bigotry. With the gift of freedom and consciousness came the disillusioning fact of Eden. Men and women were blessed with reason and skill, the power to choose life or make incredible blunders. As we look closer at human nature and observe our behavior, we find that people make conscious decisions that can have only destructive consequences. Why?

For centuries before Christ, many great Jewish thinkers reflected on this and called it Sin, the natural tendency in people to choose what they wanted rather than what the community as a whole needed or what the laws of God required. With the advent and progress of psychology over the past 100 years, we have fresh evidence that there is an innate inclination in man to make choices that will increase his or her own sense of comfort and security before he or she thinks of the outcome for others. Consequently, when the needs of others are severely handicapped, violence and alienation inevitably result: it is not only I who is looking out for "Number One," but everyone else, too.

In our discussion of a psychology of religion in this chapter, we will look at the forces of good and evil in man and see how they are always bound to the institutions within which we live. We will first examine the earthly realm before turning to the Faith dimension in Chapter Four.

The Battlefield

At the purely human level, as we develop and grow spiritually on our individual journeys through life, each of us experiences simultaneous pulls toward our creative and destructive sides. There are three such forces pulling us in opposite directions:

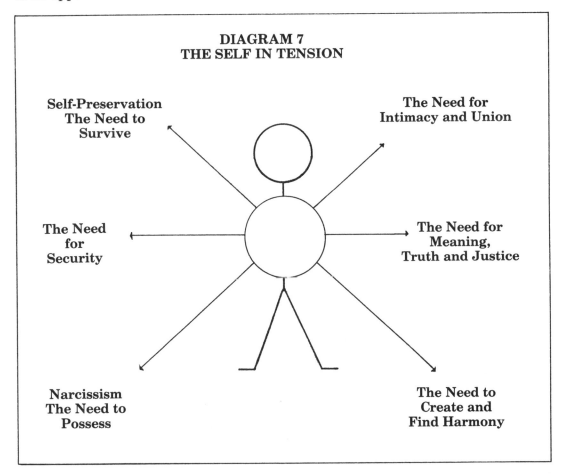

DIAGRAM 7
THE SELF IN TENSION

Self-Preservation
The Need to
Survive

The Need for
Intimacy and Union

The Need
for
Security

The Need for
Meaning,
Truth and Justice

Narcissism
The Need to
Possess

The Need to
Create and
Find Harmony

1. Self-preservation vs. Harmony and Creativity
2. Security vs. Truth and Justice
3. Narcissism vs. Intimacy and Union

Diagram 7 illustrates the tensions each of us experiences throughout life. They are felt at the center of ourselves which we call the Self, a place of pure self-consciousness. There are three such tensions: between self-preservation and survival and the need for creativity and harmony, between security and the need for comfort and control and the need for meaning and justice; and between narcissism and the desire to be at the center of everything and the need for intimacy and love. To understand these polarities better we must examine our definition of self and the concept of journey. What exactly is self?

Many psychologists and spiritual writers believe that our gift of reflective consciousness is the Self. Dr. Frank Kimper puts it this way:

> By self I mean the sheer beingness of a being—not his body, not his mind, not his life-style, not his relationship to his environment, not his beliefs, values or assumptions, but just pure consciousness of being—just pure life thrusting in a number of directions, just pure willing. And when I speak of 'pure willing' in this connection I am not referring to a passive state of 'being willing' but to an active, aggressive willing to be—an energized thrust toward being in which, again, 'being' is not to be thought of as a passive state suggested perhaps by such statements as "I just 'am' ", or "He just 'is' " as in though 'isness' could be equated with 'inertness.' No, the self is the center of dynamic becoming, in which the word 'dynamic' is to be understood in its simple dictionary sense as 'energy' in motion, effecting and directing change. So, the 'self' is a dynamic center of being, a center of consciousness, actively willing change in the direction of becoming the free and individual entity one is potentially.
>
> (Frank Kimper. Self and Therapy. An unpublished paper.)

This self, this center of consciousness, discovers itself at inception as not only being in life, but also in tension. On the one hand it wants to achieve its fullest potential while on the other it needs to preserve its very existence. This has led some psychologists, such as Kimper, to conclude that the central motivation of each self is self-preservation. Others, such as Kurt Goldstein and Abraham Maslow, see the self's motivation as self-actualization. Both motives, of course, are present and are experienced as a tension between preserving the self on the one hand and becoming a creative force on the other. The great spiritual traditions have described this as a tension between the need "to be" and the need "to become."

In diagram 7, this tension is somewhat more complex. Self-preservation is actually three distinct tensions of self-preservation, security, and the proclivity toward narcissism. The other side of the tension, self-actualization, is actually made up of the three distinct opposite needs for creativity, meaning, and intimacy. When these are exaggerated they become a battlefield within each of us between good and evil.

Journey

These polarities within are fairly easy to understand when we realize that each of us is a pilgrim in a state of continual development. Recent advances in the understanding of personality have confirmed what the traditions had intuited and spoken of for centuries—that each life is developmental and marked by clear stages of development. Although this development can in part be regarded as natural given a friendly and supportive environment, it also requires discipline if one is to reach exceptional levels of spiritual growth.

The traditional levels of spiritual development which Saint Bonaventure called the Stages of Ascent concentrated on discipline that enabled exceptional growth and the experience of union with God. Recent advances in psychosocial development emphasize that negative or damaging experiences in growing up can actually stunt or prevent growth. In fact, many psychologists suggest that since life is rarely perfect, we need help in the natural process of growing up. Guidance counselors, for example, are common in most school systems. The point is that discipline and nurturance of our gifts is necessary at all stages of our growth process.

When we look at the Stages of Ascent that Bonaventure speaks of and compare it with, for example, the work of Sigmund Freud or Carl Rogers, it is difficult to see similarities. Can they really be talking about the same thing? Though both speak of development, they are dealing with different chunks of the developmental scale. Consider a measurement of life development as a scale of one to ten:

1.— — — — — — — — — — — — — → 5. — — — — — — — — — — — — — — →10.

Psychologists and mental health professionals generally work with people from 1 to 5. The writers in the spiritual traditions like Bonaventure work with people in stages from 5 up to 10 and even beyond. Although it is the same scale and similar methods are often used to aid a person, the goals and consequences are quite different. The psychologist is concerned with helping a person become an emotionally healthy and productive member of society. The traditional spiritual guide is concerned with that only as a starting point in a person's greater realization of his maximum potential as a child of God.

Let us look closer at psychosocial development. Erik Erikson, a modern psychologist and anthropologist and a follower of Sigmund Freud, posits eight stages necessary for healthy development from birth to death:

Stage One: Basic Trust vs. Mistrust. In this stage a baby must experience initial warmth and care from his mother to grow up with a healthy attitude toward others. It is the groundwork of the capacity for Faith later on.

Stage Two: Autonomy vs. Shame and Doubt. Between the ages of two and approximately five years the child must receive sufficient positive reinforcement from the parents to gain a sense of self-control without losing self-esteem. This involves such steps as toilet training and learning how to walk.

Stage Three: Initiative vs. Guilt. As the child learns language, goes to school, and begins to deal with the differences of his or her parents, he confronts the limits of his or her skills and the limits of behavior in a wider social sphere. Depending upon the negative or positive effects of this confrontation, guilt may or may not result.

Stage Four: Industry vs. Inferiority. It is hoped that the child is now enthusiastic about learning and becoming productive and is interested in his or her own projects. Support is needed to insure that this is a positive rather than a negative experience.

Stage Five: Identity vs. Identity Diffusion. Although there are three more stages, this is the most critical for Erikson and, in a sense, the apex. This is because a sense of personal identity occurs in a person 18 years or older only when he or she has been able to integrate in a healthy way the previous stages, an integration that sustains the person throughout his or her life. Major life changes occur at this stage such as going to college or finding a job, leaving home, getting married and starting a family. Success at this stage depends on one's ability to trust others and act with autonomy, initiative, and productivity. These three skills now reoccur in the following three stages.

Stage Six: Intimacy and Solidarity vs. Isolation. This refers to marriage and all adult relationships. The capacity for intimacy rests upon the previous integration of basic trust of others.

Stage Seven: Generativity vs. Stagnation. As middle age approaches and a person realizes he or she will not be president or the world's greatest author, the result will be either continued productivity and happiness or stagnation, depending upon the strength of the early stages of initiative, autonomy, and industry.

Stage Eight: Integration vs. Despair. This stage, dependent clearly for Erikson on previous integrations, can lead to either the productive and happy process of aging or a fear of death and the experience of despair.

The goal of the psychological staging process is emotional maturity and stability so that the person is able to choose and actualize a productive and happy life and be a contributor rather than a distractor in society. Carl Rogers, a major contributor to modern counseling practice, spoke of the values and high points of the process as follows:

> Perhaps more than all else, the client comes to value an openness to all of his inner and outer experience. To be open to and sensitive to his own inner reactions and feelings, the reactions and feelings of others, and the realities of

the objective world—this is a direction which he clearly prefers. This openness becomes the client's most valued resource.

(Rogers. *Freedom to Learn*, p. 259.)

This experience of the mature man or woman is also the foundation for what the great traditions in spirituality have called Conversion, which for them was most commonly the first stage in their view of development or spiritual ascent.

The Spiritual Journey

A number of writers have placed before us spiritual road maps, stages of the development of man's spiritual consciousness. Let us return to and examine the schema suggested by Saint Bonaventure.

Bonaventure was a 13th century friar, a professor at the University of Paris, and the chief executive of the Franciscan Order. One of his works was *The Life of Saint Francis*. He was only a boy when Saint Francis died. In this book, which is of pivotal importance, Bonaventure synthesized all the spiritual traditions of western Christianity up to that time. His view of spiritual development still predominates today. It is no coincidence that he wrote about the life of Saint Francis, the most ecumenically satisfying of Christian heroes because of his radical attempt to imitate the values and lifestyle of Jesus of Nazareth. His method, the most extreme in western Christian history, and heavily tainted with an Italian medieval flavor, was very significant. For his part, Bonaventure played anthropologist not only in recording Francis' journey, but in illustrating how it exemplified the stages of spiritual development.

Saint Francis' major contribution to western spirituality was his emphasis on poverty, an expression of radical *detachment* from worldly things. Like Francis, by being unattached to anxiety, to material wants and needs, and to any other thing that dominates or possesses us, we are free to grow in self-actualizing ways and reach perfection as sons and daughters of God. This same detachment is central to the healing process of the modern psychologist.

Bonaventure posits that Francis went through four stages of spiritual development: Conversion, Purgation, Illumination, and Perfection. Let us look at these individually.

1. Conversion. This first stage took place when Francis was a "young boy," probably approaching his teenage years. At that time he lived in a fairly wealthy setting, busy with the internal affairs of his father's business. Upon recovery from a sudden physical illness, he left home to become a knight. His life changed after seeing a vision in which God asked him to be a knight in the service of the Lord. He gave up the need for self-preservation (what knighthood meant in those days), renounced the need for security (working in his father's merchant clothing business), and for the power and control that would have come with the success of the business. (See the three tensions of the self in diagram 7.)

2. *Purgation.* At this stage of his life, Francis explored austerity. He ate very little, dressed shabbily, prayed constantly, and paid attention to his treatment of others, especially the downtrodden. In essence, Purgation is the discipline necessary to carry through with the values and gifts a person has decided to follow and nurture in life. For Francis this was a radical departure from the life he had known.

3. *Illumination.* In this period of his life, Francis felt a heightened sense and experience of the divine presence. This is seen by all the major religious writers in mysticism as "Gift." The person is swept along by the values and priorities he or she seeks, literally becoming energized by them. Along with this evolves personal insight into the call and direction of their ministry. Their ministry is confirmed within and becomes quite evident to their community. Their new behavior and skills are a clear confirmation of their specific call to a ministry of Shepherd Leadership. For example, Francis felt he should go to Syria to convert the followers of Islam. He made a significant impression but converted no one and thus concluded that this was not appropriate to his call. His ministry was to be at home in Italy with his community.

4. *Perfection.* Writers later called this the "Unitive Way," the experience of at-oneness with God. Perfection in its essence is the ability of the human being to develop his or her gifts and talents to their maximum potential within the context of given limitations. One of Saint Francis' severe limitations was his mistreatment of his own body which in the end killed him. (He did live 43 years, however, which was quite old for his day.) Another limitation was his lack of administrative skills which became a problem as his order grew and began to espouse values contrary to his own calling. Despite all of this, he reached the stage called Perfection which, we have noted, does not mean he was perfect in all things. Rather, it meant that he lived with such an intense presence of God that he began to see the world through divine eyes with all the power that comes with it. This was expressed externally as well as internally. For example, he experienced the marks of the cross on his body, the stigmata, and there were reports of his ability to heal. He established an Order of Married People dedicated to his view of the Christ-ly life that virtually ended much of the feudal warring of mercenary knights in Europe. (As this "Third Order" expanded, fewer people were willing to take up arms, regardless of the rewards.)

The Institutional Communal Connection

We noted earlier that if all possible human development were on a scale of one to ten, psychosocial development would deal with one through five and spiritual development as portrayed in the traditions, five through ten. It would be a simple continuum. The astute reader will observe, however, that there must be other differences. In current psychology, the ultimate human person is mature, capable of making choices, and has overcome adolescent identity crises. Spiritual traditions begin with the concept of Conversion. Do they converge with psychosocial traditions at this point?

It was precisely questions like this that brought into being the discipline of psychology of religion at the turn of this century. The most celebrated work on the psychology of religion is *The Varieties of Religious Experience* by William James. The book, which is still used as a text, is the series of Gifford lectures in natural religion given in Edinburgh in 1900–1901. A number of persons, James among them, had noticed a strong similarity between the resolution of the crises of adolescence and the Conversion experience. Religious revivals and tent meetings were prominent in the United States at the time and many researchers began to study the matter seriously. One man, E. T. Clark, collected data from 2,174 cases. He observed that in both adolescent crises and religious conversion, clear stages of resolution could be traced: the subject moved from an initial unhappy circumstance to a strong emotional experience or crisis, to greater insight or illumination, and finally to a prolonged behavioral change and adherence to a different set of values. Upon examination of the experience of Saint Francis, who was an adolescent at the time of his conversion, one can see all of these elements.

Further research finally highlighted certain differences. E. T. Clark's work revealed that only 6.7 percent of his 2,174 subjects had sudden conversions; the others occurred over a prolonged period of time. In addition, resolution of the crises did not always bring persons closer to God or to those values which are other-oriented, as religious values are. These discoveries have led Walter Houston Clark to define religious conversion as

> That type of spiritual growth or development which involves an appreciable change of direction concerning religious ideas and behavior. Most clearly and typically it denotes an emotional episode of illuminating suddenness, which may be deep or superficial, though it may also come about by a more gradual process.
>
> (*The Psychology of Religion,* p. 191.)

The problem is not resolved, however, because the connection is not complete. We must turn to the roots of Western tradition—the Bible. When the Old Testament refers to spiritual development, it addresses the community of the people of God who are engaged in their journey. Individuals are important but always within an institutional context. Israel's journey involves a rabble brought out of Egypt to the edge of the promised land by Moses. Other leaders and prophets continue the pastoral call. In and through this process the people grow and the ministry of individuals is clarified. Law-oriented, the process has a strong external component—salvation community journeying through history. It is a magnificent vision.

With the arrival of Jesus of Nazareth, a strong interpersonal concern for each individual and an emphasis on the inner life are introduced. Jesus is concerned for the poor and the abandoned and he speaks of God as a personal loving Father. At the same time, however, he called the twelve into a community which later became the Church, an institution both heavenly and earthly.

Saint Paul extended the vision, placing strong emphasis on the community as the Body of Christ with each of us contributing our unique gifts and ministry. From these examples, we can see that Christian ministry and human growth always occur within an institutional setting, within the context of the community of salvation. Conversion, then, unlike the integrative experience arising purely from identity crises (adolescent or otherwise), takes place within the context of a supportive community. One is called forth by that community to a life-long relationship with its author, Christ as Lord.

Psychosocial development (one to five on our scale) is more individual in nature. As we continue on the scale of development into the stages of spiritual ascent (five to ten on the scale), growth is more consciously communal in nature. Francis, at his period of Conversion, started a new religious community, the Friars Minor, which became a support system to him for the rest of his life. He did not experience growth alone. Our scale now appears as follows:

1.	5.	10.
Healthy Emotional Development	**Spiritually Healthy Development**	
Individuals in Institutions	**Mutual System/Person Development**	

Before we continue, two points must be noted. First, we place Conversion at the middle of the continuum (5 above). Schemas like this are limited for the purposes of communication. Very often a radical conversion occurs well before this, propelling a person forward in exceptional growth. The identity crisis period in normal emotional growth is *not* Conversion, but it is the condition and setting for it. As such it is something the spiritual guide needs to be aware of.

Secondly, institutions are part of a person's growth over the entire continuum and are thus essential to our growth. In the first half of the scale they are a necessary adversary while in the second half they are essential if human growth is to continue. If that growth is to be positive and life-giving, the institution must become a friend rather than an adversary. In order to advance beyond five on our scale in a healthy, morally integrated way, a leader needs positive system support. We will deal with this last point in detail later in Chapter III. We are now ready to address directly the question of our life-long struggle between good and evil.

3. | The Struggle

Unamuno, in speaking of the necrophilous character of the cry, "Long live death," touched upon the core of the problem of evil. There is no more fundamental distinction between men, psychologically and morally, than the one between those who love death, and those who love life. What matters here, as always in living phenomena, is which trend is the stronger, so that it determines man's behavior— not the complete absence or presence of one of the two orientations.

(Fromm. *The Heart of Man,* p. 37)

Introduction

Through the gift of consciousness, the human being has the potential to reach the stars. This has been the message of the mystics and sages of all ages. To reach the heights of spiritual development requires discipline and struggle, for at each point of growth we are pulled in two directions: to Narcissism on the one hand and taking authority for the created order on the other. We experience this pull as a force between the destructive and creative sides of ourselves. Viewed overall, these become scales of development as illustrated in the following diagram.

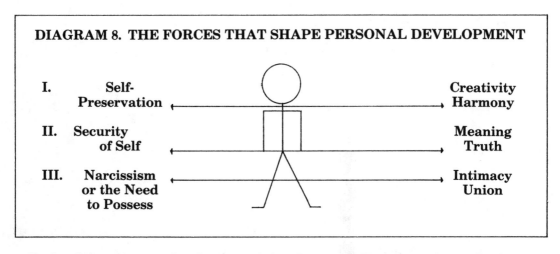

DIAGRAM 8. THE FORCES THAT SHAPE PERSONAL DEVELOPMENT

I.   Self-Preservation   Creativity / Harmony

II.   Security of Self   Meaning / Truth

III.   Narcissism or the Need to Possess   Intimacy / Union

Each of these is a scale of personal development. For example, each of us moves from a need for self-preservation, security and control to the pursuit of creativity, meaning in our lives, and intimacy. Yet at the same time, wherever we are in our development, we experience the pull to preserve our selves, to be secure, and to totally control. Each of these scales has a very personal dimension as well as an even stronger system or institutional dimension. Why stronger? At the institutional level, all three dimensions become related as a powerful coercive force to good or to evil. To understand this, we must first examine each dimension separately.

I. The Forces to Preserve and to Create

The personal dimension of this first scale will be clearer when we are aware of the values between the two poles of self-preservation and creativity.

DIAGRAM 9				
Self-Preservation The Need to survive	**Family**	**Work/** Competence	**Service/** Vocation	**Being Self** Creativity	**Ecority*** The Need to Create The Will for Harmony

*Ecority is the personal authority to use technology to bring about a harmony between man and nature (Ecology).

Survival, one of the most rudimentary aspects of all animal life, refers to adaption to the demands and requirements of nature. It is the defense, protection and sustenance of one's very existence. As one's life appears to be more and more in danger, there is an inner need to do everything necessary to preserve it. This is why we tend to be most self-centered when we are struggling to survive.

An example of this is a family engaged in divorce proceedings. The wife might say, "I loved him once, but now I've got 'Number One' to think about. I have the kids to care for, and suppose he doesn't make the payments?" Another example is the executive under pressure who has no support group. He comes home at night worn out, his mind full of tomorrow's decisions, and his son wants help with his homework. To make things worse, his wife comes home one hour late for supper which she forgot to prepare because she is a busy professional also. Fifteen minutes after coming in the door they are ready to begin World War III, each trying to survive at the expense of the other.

In diagram 9, self-preservation proceeds to family and work. As we grow and mature, we soon recognize that we need others in order to survive, another rudimentary fact of living in society. The 'Family' is the basic unit of society. People need one another to survive in a civilized order. Family is the place where love is nurtured, but it is also an extension of the need to survive.

At the most basic level, work is "doing and producing" in order to provide the necessities of life for the family and myself. By modifying the environment, we are liberated from nature at one level but actually re-create nature at another level. We take a raw material of the natural world such as petroleum, make plastics with it and from that, half the products we use daily. We have fiberglass boats, plastic car seats and shoes and even plastic lenses in our eyeglasses. Work, then, is modifying nature and doing and producing what is necessary to survive and be with each other (family) in a quality way. Family and work are therefore on the same continuum as self-preservation.

Moving to the right side of the diagram we see the values of Service/Vocation, Being Self/Creativity, and Ecority and the need to Create. As a person matures, the positive aspects of family and work as a sense of one's own competence combine with the innate need in each of us to be creative. This need pulls us from the other end of the continuum away from the emphasis on survival needs. From family comes the experience of being myself and the will to create my own family and my own world. Work and the sense of my own competence now moves beyond simply doing things to survive to the will to be independent and do what I want to do. This is the emergence of work as vocation and service.

At the far right of the continuum we encounter the need in each of us to create, that aspect of us that is, in a sense, created in the image of God. Just as God is Creator, so we have within us that same creative urge. This need is related to the value of ecority and the will for harmony. What does this mean?

Ecology is the concern for overall harmony between humans and the rest of our natural living environment. Ecority is the value of ecology combined with a sense of personal authority and the use of technology. It means care for the natural created order by using technology and personal power in a responsible way. Ecority is creativity at the global level, seeing man as a global family

reated order as our responsibility as co-creators with God. Man
he "chief gardener."

he purposes of family is to procreate. It is where each of us finds
urturance. Thus equipped, we are able to join in the spiritual life
with the vision of becoming a co-creator and caring for the family of man
instead of surviving only in our immediate family. Family also allows us to
become what we really want to be. Through its love, the nurturing family
provides the opportunity for a person to experience sufficient affirmation to
move beyond self needs and begin to see work as service to others. As the need
for creativity is stimulated, this work becomes not just any work, but the kind
of work I like to do and with which I can make a positive contribution. Work
becomes vocation and again my need for creative expression is enhanced.

Finally, contained in this pull to be creative is also the will, and to some
extent, the need for harmony. After we create something, whether a family, a
painting, or a management plan, its effectiveness depends on internal
consistency. Harmony goes hand-in-hand with the act of creating. There are
many levels of harmony; ecority is harmony exercised at the highest level. It
is not only internal harmony, but harmony among all things in the natural
order. At one end of the scale is self-preservation and its often negative
consequences of war, personal alienation, and pillaging of natural resources.
At the other end of the scale pulling in the opposite direction is the need to
create and the possibility of personal and global harmony rather than chaos.

II. The Need for Security
and the Pursuit of Truth

In this second dimension, the conflict is between the need for security,
comfort, and control, and the need for Meaning and Truth. Between these two
poles are other values we need to be aware of. They are illustrated in diagram
10.

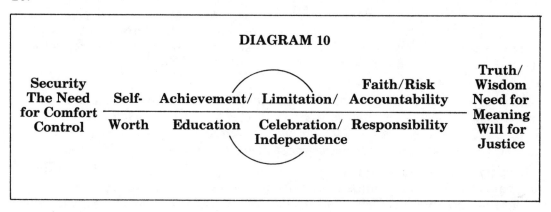

The majority of writers link security with the need for self-preservation, an
obvious and strong connection. Having "won the war" we feel secure. What is

not so obvious is that security is a unique motivational force. Self-preservation is the legitimate reaction to an externally perceived threat while security is an internal feeling of comfort and non-threat. When my life is threatened, my natural reaction is to defend or fight back to preserve myself, but when I am in a state of constant insecurity I become more controlling. The distinction is subtle during a period of crisis, but as I mature the differences become clearer.

Security can be understood better by discussing its counterpart, insecurity, the feeling of anxiety each of us experiences. Anxiety is worry about the future, the belief that "something negative is going to happen, but I do not know what it is." Fear, on the other hand, is reaction to a clearly perceived threat when my very survival is at stake. Imagine, for example, that you are on one of Christopher Columbus' ships voyaging to discover the New World. After ten weeks at sea, the supplies are dwindling and you are worried about the future. Even with a steady wind and good health, you are worried. This is anxiety, the feeling of insecurity. Now suppose a storm should arise. Out of fear and the instinct of self-preservation, you fight to defend your very existence. This is the subtle difference between fear and anxiety.

Though anxiety and insecurity are part of the normal state of being and a natural result of expectations about the future, the presence of too much anxiety can be a problem. The more anxious we are, the less comfortable and more controlling we become. If we feel that a survival situation is at hand, we worry more about the future and become more controlling. The point is that security, comfort, and control are interconnected. Let us now look at this in a more natural and positive light.

Security is the feeling of internal comfort each of us feels. In a sense, it is the pursuit of happiness. To be in control feels good and comfortable. One has only to look at American automobile advertising over the last several years to see examples of this. Consider an expensive import car such as the Mercedes. Its foreign-sponsored advertisers point to its engineering and performance. Contrast this with the advertising of an American prestige car such as the Cadillac or Lincoln Mercury. No matter how well engineered it is, the emphasis is on overall looks and the luxurious interior, not to mention the computerized controls. Comfort is stressed, and by implication, security. This kind of advertising has worked in America because the affluent want and are motivated by these desires. Equally fascinating in such advertising is the way luxury and comfort are always linked to prestige. Achievement is an extension of security and comfort, one naturally begetting the other. If one buys an expensive car, a Cadillac or Porsche, people will look up to you as a successful person, an achiever.

Looking at diagram 10 above, we see that as we grow and mature, security evolves into self-worth and finally achievement/education. What is the connection? During the time from conception to birth, as we rest in the ultimate security and comfort in our mother's womb and later in her arms, each of us learns that "I am worth a great deal." The whole world fulfills my needs and wants. This very positive feeling is my initial sense of worth. Not only am I of great value, but I enjoy the feeling of comfort and security.

As I mature, I soon realize that I live in a social world. In addition to "me" there are mother, father, and many others who are also worthwhile. Self-worth is a social value, the feeling that "When they know me well, others will discover that I am of great value." It does not mean that only I think I am great, but that others will discover it, too, when they get to know me. Self-worth is social in nature. Persons with a low sense of self-worth or self-esteem are therefore insecure about what significant others think about them.

There is another side to self-worth which stems from curiosity or the need to know about things around me. The knowledge that others are valuable spawns in us from the very beginning of life a natural curiosity to understand the world outside. This aspect of self-worth pulls from the other end of the continuum to a desire to discover the meaning of life and to seek Truth. We thus move across the continuum to discover the values of achievement and education as extensions of worth. Again, as I mature, I need to feel worthwhile in my accomplishments. By achieving in work and school, I experience myself as valuable to others and society as a whole. Education trains me to do this. More than the minimal training for a secure future, however, education is also an introduction to the pursuit of knowledge for its own sake. Achievement can become a fanatical need to succeed without regard for others, and education can become education-for-certification only to advance me in my job. However, if I mature spiritually, I move beyond this to the right side of our diagram.

The time comes in our lives (referred to earlier as Conversion) when we are seized once again by the higher values in the continuum. Motivated now by the need for Meaning and Truth more than the need for security, we actually become insecure when these new expressions of base needs are not met. After achievement/education on the right side, we reach Independence and Faith/Risk and Accountability as we approach the needs for Meaning and Truth.

As I achieve, succeed, and become knowledgeable in my chosen field of work, there comes a point where I want to test my own creativity and independence. This juncture in one's development marks a new sense of personal authority. It is a point where one's conscience for the first time is fully formed and where decisions as to what is right and wrong take on a new significance. We have a new sense of our own authority as independent thinking persons. It is a time of experimentation, growth, and also greater awareness of one's limitations.

Many times during consultation with a corporation I have heard, "I have been with this corporation for ten years and they have treated me very well. But I do not agree with a lot of their policies. They have offered me more money to stay but that just won't do it for me. I have got to move out on my own just to see what I can do." For others this decisive point has meant exciting but uncertain change that required transcendence of insecurity. A nun in her mid-forties told me, "I joined this community twenty-five years ago and dedicated my life to God which for me meant being a nurse in a general hospital because that is what our sisters did. But now I want to use those skills differently. I am not sure what that means; perhaps it means doing nothing for a while until God tells me what is right for me at this time." She was growing, recognizing her limits, and even beginning to celebrate them.

The sudden sense of new life and new direction is an experience of being *grasped by the future* as new possibilities are opened to a person. Its sure sign is the insistence on independence and the authority of self-directedness. More often than not, it is also a time of search for new meaning in one's life. Another important aspect at this stage of development is the new-found sense of equality and justice that emerges. The person acquires a greater sense of others' rights. If my new sense of independence is to grow, I must recognize my own equality and right to independence. This heightened awareness of others' equality and rights is also a result of the openness to the future because it is itself a pursuit of the truth and justice we all seek. Erich Fromm put it this way:

> Summing up, love for life will develop most in a society where there is: Security in the sense that the basic material conditions for a dignified life are not threatened, Justice in the sense that nobody can be an end for the purposes of another, and Freedom in the sense that each man has the possibility to be an active and responsible member of society.
> *(The Heart of Man: Its Genius for Good and Evil,* p. 57)

Beyond Independence and Limitation/Celebration we now encounter Faith/Risk, Accountability/Responsibility, and research, or the pursuit of knowledge. Paul Tillich once said that the excessive need for security and control is a state of unfaith. Faith-as-risk, the opposite of security, is the experience of actually celebrating or acting on my limitations and talents. We will deal more with the question of faith in the next chapter. For our purposes at this point, faith is the radical sense of risking and consciously venturing beyond one's own security needs for the sake of chosen values in the pursuit of meaning and truth.

The sense of independence one feels at this stage of maturity can often regress to an inordinate need for comfort and power. If the love of my newfound independence does not develop into a radical awareness of the need not only to recognize the independence of others but to cooperate with others with renewed depth, then it returns to an even stronger form of isolation and individualized power. When this happens, the need for control and security once again predominates. Recognition of one's limitations is thus essential, for it allows us to celebrate our need to move beyond independence to *inter*dependence. When a person exceeds the sense of personal independence, he or she grows by recognizing that real freedom occurs only as we form community and support systems that nurture the individuality of everyone.

This takes not only risk but faith in the goodness and potential of others. I have to trust others as much as I trust myself. For this reason, accountability and mutual responsibility are important at this level of development. Faith in each other requires that we be mutually accountable to each other. It is the communal recognition of limitation as a positive value.

It has been my experience that persons who have had a bad experience in institutions and lack management skills and understanding often react so much against institutionalism that they become very self-centered upon encountering the independence stage. They never reach the experience of faith and risk I described. This has been particularly true of persons in the professional religious ministry such as members of religious communities. It is not unusual, for example, to find a member of a religious community living alone in an apartment and working in a local parish while refusing to associate with the community. A sister recently said to me, "I lived under those rigid rules for twenty years and I will have no more of it. I like my apartment and I am doing the Lord's work, so they should just leave me alone." I pointed out to her that the community was not operating under those rigid rules any more. Her reply was that she no longer trusted them, she was tired of risking, and she was very comfortable and secure where she was. A vision of what community could be was obviously absent.

When one does grow in faith and begins to cooperate at new levels with others, one's knowledge of the world grows tremendously. Trusting others and affirming their worth as being as valuable as my own is a loving act. Simone Weil shows how this is actually the pursuit of truth:

> Pure and genuine love always desires above all to dwell wholly in the truth whatever it may be, unconditionally. Every other sort of love desires before anything else means of satisfaction, and for this reason is a source of error and falsehood. Pure and genuine love is in itself spirit of truth. It is the Holy Spirit. The Greek word which is translated "spirit" means literally "fiery breath," breath mingled with fire, and it represented, in antiquity, the notion which science represents today by the word "energy." What we translate by "spirit of truth" signifies the energy of truth, truth as an active force. Pure love is this active force, the love which will not at any price, under any conditions, have anything to do with either falsehood or error.
>
> ("Truth and Love," *A Diary of Readings* by John Baillie.)

Thus, at one end of the scale we need security while at the other we need the security that comes from knowing and understanding what life, specifically my life, is about. To know what my life means is to discover its *meaning*. Viktor Frankl speaks of the pull towards meaning as follows:

> Man's search for meaning is a primary force in his life and not a secondary rationalization of instinctual drives. This meaning is unique and specific in that it must and can be fulfilled by him alone; only then does it achieve a significance that will satisfy his own will to meaning.
>
> (*Man's Search for Meaning*, p. 154.)

The desire for justice at this level is also a part of this pursuit of truth and wisdom; it inspires us to act on the truth perceived as a benefit to our fellow man and helps to insure societal security.

III. *Narcissism and the need for Intimacy*

In this third scale, tension exists between our need for power and our simultaneous need for love. Because it builds on the knowledge of the previous scales, it is the most potent of the three. It is illustrated in diagram 11.

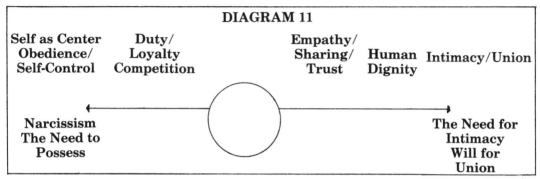

Literature through the ages has shown us that people have recognized the tendency in themselves to feel they are the center of the universe and that everyone should cater to their needs. One of the earliest accounts from which the word narcissism comes is in the ancient Greek myth of Echo and Narcissus in which a self-centered youth, Narcissus, cruelly shuns the love of the nymph, Echo. One day while sitting by a pool of water he sees his image reflected in the water. Thinking the reflection that of another nymph, he falls in love with it. Unable to have the person whose beauty he loved, he pined away and finally faded from existence. In his place grew a flower, purple within and white without, which forever commemorates his memory.

Narcissism is a force within each of us quite distinct from survival and security needs. Aaron Stern in a little book called *Me: The Narcissistic American* wrote:

> When the security of survival is attained, it provides man—and society—with time to pause and ponder the meaning of life. He begins to search for purpose and, as a part of purpose, pleasure. He begins seeking more of those special moments in the sun. (p. 2)

Erich Fromm described narcissism even more strongly: "Narcissism is a passion the intensity of which can only be compared with sexual desire and the desire to stay alive. In fact, many times it proves to be stronger than either." (*The Heart of Man*, p. 85)

Infants are only aware of the reality that they exist and have needs for food, warmth, and bodily contact; they think they are the centers of the world. It is a natural state of narcissism. Indeed, if my parents do not see me as the center I would probably not survive. What is very positive about this state of infancy and fascinating from a theological point of view is that it is an experience of being of "infinite worth," our first awareness of God's grace. The experience of being of infinite value introduces us at the onset of life to the gospel, the good news that each of us is of infinite value in the eyes of God. The experience of Conversion is simply a conscious reaffirmation of this fact.

Narcissism becomes possession, as we shall see in more detail later, when we fail to recognize that all people are of the same infinite worth. When we develop naturally, however, we soon realize that if our demands for attention are to be met, some restraint is necessary. We thus learn to do as we are told for our own good, and we learn the necessity of discipline. In short, looking at our diagram, we learn obedience and self-control.

As we continue to grow, we learn this same lesson with the wider range of peers and superiors we encounter at school and our place of work. We learn duty and loyalty to our friends, to our primary institutions, and to our country. Ever-present, however, is our basic inclination toward narcissism and sense of our ultimate worth. Deep down this is the feeling of grandiosity we all have which emerges as the natural need to be competitive.

Like the early experience of narcissism, competition has its positive side of confronting us with our limitations and training us to see the values of others. It enables us to find our place and develop hitherto latent skills to their maximum potential. Training for the Olympics is an example of this. On the negative side, competition can actually reinforce early feelings of narcissism and convince the winner that he or she is superior to other human beings. At each and every point, it would seem that we can either grow spiritually or run the risk of regressing.

At the midpoint, a possible conversion occurs as once again the person is grasped by the other end of the continuum, in this case the need for intimacy. Intimacy and union are the highest expressions of what we normally call love, which is pure selfless giving to another, the exact opposite of narcissism. At this point of conversion, the ability to be dutiful and loyal for my own sake becomes the need to share with others what I am at a deeper level. My grandiosity exercised in my competitive spirit is now modified as I appreciate myself enough to share it more deeply with others. At the same time, my maturity allows me to recognize the beauty present in others. Consequently, feelings and imagination become important. I now begin to share and listen in depth; I begin to trust others.

The central skill elicited from this process is that of empathy, the ability to project my imagination into the imaginations of others. In doing so, they are able to see themselves with more clarity having been with me. It is the precursor to human dignity, the next value on the scale. This value of empathy was the unique sign of the man Jesus of Nazareth: he entered the imagination of the poor in the Sermon on the Mount; he entered the imagination of each of the Apostles as he called them; he entered the imagination of the adulteress when he prevented her stoning; and he entered the imagination of each of us when he gave his life for us on the cross. His presence among us allowed us to see ourselves more clearly. In doing so he dignified the human race.

The final point on the scale is selfless giving in the act of intimacy that we all seek. Intimacy in its highest form between lovers brings with it a sense of union. We speak of the union between husband and wife as prefiguring the union between man and God which the mystics constantly spoke of as the very purpose of their lives. Evelyn Underhill notes that for the mystic it was not a need for union but for a lifetime of exceptional discipline; it is the will for union:

> The mystics find the basis for their method not in logic but in life: in the existence of a discoverable "real," a spark of true being, within the seeking subject, which can, in that ineffable experience which they call the "act of union," fuse itself with and thus apprehend the reality of the sought Object. In theoretical language, their theory of knowledge is that the spirit of man, itself essentially divine, is capable of immediate communion with God, the One Reality.
>
> (*Mysticism: A Study in the Nature and Development of Man's Spiritual Consciousness*, p. 24)

What is particularly interesting about mystics is that when they reached these heights of union, celibate as many of them were, their capacity for intimacy with their friends also increased. Intimacy between each of us as human beings is thus a precondition for these higher experiences of union that are beyond the reach of most of us.

Intermediate Conclusions

Up to this point we have examined three scales, each a battleground between the natural inclinations within us to be more self-centered and yet open to others and society. At one end of each scale we examined self-preservation, security, and narcissism, and at the other the forces toward ecority and harmony, truth and the need for meaning, and intimacy and the will for union. However, only as we see these forces as a whole do we realize their full implications. The link that unifies these seemingly separate elements is the dimension of the institution.

As mentioned in Chapter One, each of us develops in relationship to our primary institutions. We are individuals as systems rather than persons in isolation. When the need for survival, security, and narcissism are connected through institutional pressures, the force of evil is unleashed in ways that are beyond the power of the individual to cope with. On the other hand, when intimacy, truth, and harmony are connected through a loving institution or community, an equal force to the good is mobilized. These forces thus become the battleground. In order to grasp this concept we must see how the three scales appear in an institutional context. This is the subject of the next chapter.

4. ▮ The Battlefield

Then war broke out in heaven.
Michael and his angels battled against the dragon.
Although the dragon and his angels fought back, they were
overpowered and lost their place in heaven.
The huge dragon, the ancient serpent known as the devil or Satan,
the seducer of the whole world was driven out:
he was hurled down to the earth and his minions with him.

(New American Bible. Revelations, 12: 7–9)

Introduction

We have seen how in our individual struggles to grow in life-giving ways we are constantly pulled in two directions. In the last analysis, one is life-giving for ourselves and others while the opposite is securing and self-serving. This chapter is called The Battlefield, and the battlefield is institutional living.

Without institutions the civil order and all its attributes would not exist. From the institution of family emerges the possibility of love. From the institution of the church grows the declaration of the possibility of resurrection. Yet at the same time, as most of us know, institutions can be coercive, tension-producing, and destructive. Families are divorced. The church had its inquisition.

All of us live our lives within an institutional context; it is a part of who we are. The forces described in the last chapter become connected in a coercive way within the institution and create a conflict between good and evil. A narcissistic leader such as Hitler thus becomes a terrible force that affects millions. However, when an institution becomes an equally coercive force to the good, the very opposite occurs, exemplified by the church of the Acts of the Apostles. How this coercive action occurs to the good and to the evil is the subject of this chapter. The following diagram will remind us of the plan of the Battlefield.

Scale One: Institutional Construction

At the purely institutional level, work and production is the normal way we preserve ourselves on a daily basis. When a corporation's profits decrease, pressure is put on the employees to work harder and produce more. Clergy often work endless hours because their sense of worth is closely tied to their work. They rarely have a direct boss and usually try to please everyone in the congregation, which is their subtle form of survival.

As an institution grows and becomes financially secure and established so that it is able to sponsor creative opportunity for its personnel, it begins to see itself as a service to the community. Typically, the smaller the corporation whether a business or a religious community, the less attention it pays to retirement schemes or even medical coverage. As it grows, however, it can afford to invest in pension plans and even research or education, thereby promoting creativity and a range of vocational possibilities.

We see then a parallel between personal security and the emergence of vocation, creativity, and institutional support. For example, the profession of social work as we know it today did not emerge until the 19th century. Western society was not developed enough to provide this type of service for a total population. Though limited social work had been prefigured in the church for centuries as various forms of pastoral care, western civilization had to be well beyond a purely survival level to conceive of such a service as a legitimate salaried vocation.

As the institution finally becomes developed and established, it considers expansion and internal quality development. I call this Construction/New Order. In shepherd leader terms, the executive of an industry or the bishop of a diocese can now feel safe enough to raise value questions about his own system. Are we maximizing the human and spiritual development of our members? Are we really enhancing the natural environment (Ecority) and benefiting the local community?

Scale Two: Communal Accountability

On this second scale institutional security and control is promoted through administrative and management procedures. The more insecure the leadership, the more rigid the management design, a situation very similar to a small struggling family business where management is a one-person affair. Responsible controls and efficient planning are essential for any institution to develop beyond a certain point.

DIAGRAM 12
THE SYSTEM CONNECTION

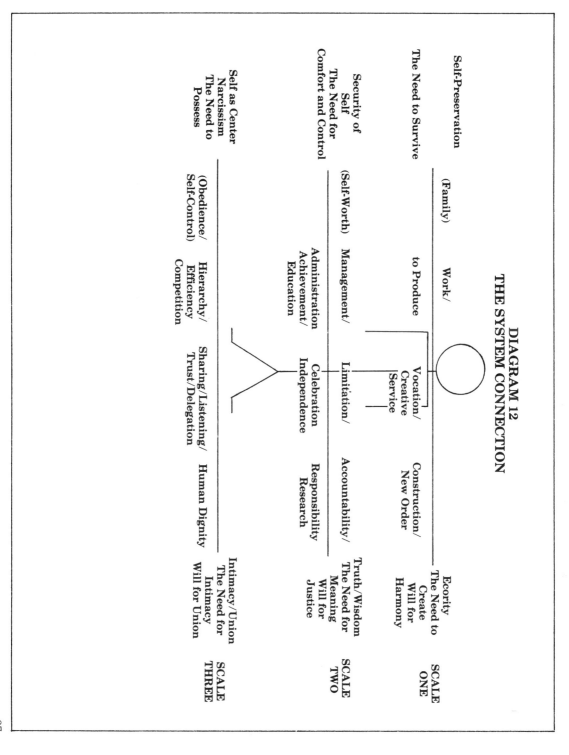

Self-Preservation

The Need to Survive

Security of
Self
The Need for
Comfort and Control

Self as Center
Narcissism
The Need to
Possess

(Family)

(Self-Worth)

(Obedience/
Self-Control)

Work/

to Produce

Management/

Administration
Achievement/
Education

Hierarchy/
Efficiency
Competition

Vocation/
Creative
Service

Limitation/

Celebration
Independence

Sharing/Listening/
Trust/Delegation

Construction/
New Order

Accountability/

Responsibility
Research

Human Dignity

Ecority
The Need to
Create
Will for
Harmony

SCALE
ONE

Truth/Wisdom
The Need for
Meaning
Will for
Justice

SCALE
TWO

Intimacy/Union
The Need for
Intimacy
Will for Union

SCALE
THREE

37

As the institution grows and security is built in through, for example, the provision of minimal benefits, the leadership can allow more independence within the ranks. More persons are given real authority. This is exemplified in the church by the development of lay ministry who have real responsibility. Restricting the role of the women in the church has been an obvious male strategy to maintain the secure system. We men, married and celibate alike, need to be cared for by "our" women. Permitting more independence requires a realistic and healthy attitude towards the institution's limitations, an attitude lacking in many churches. Few parishes in the Protestant churches, for example, accept a woman as chief pastor.

Allowing independent development demands faith and risk as well as mutual responsibility. The ultimate exercise of one's authority involves the cultivation of new ideas. Thus, institutional authority as a system of respect requires study, scholarship, and research in the pursuit of truth and the struggle for meaning and justice. For example, the question of priesthood for women in the Episcopal and Roman Catholic churches has prompted a tremendous amount of research into issues of authority and human rights. Are the rights of women being overlooked? This is a question of justice that attacks the very basic beliefs of many in the church.

Scale Three: Institution and Human Dignity

In institutions narcissism is often the natural consequence of being in a leadership position. The person at the top sees the whole system and has to make decisions from that standpoint while representing the system to the rest of society. It is very easy at this level to conclude that "only I have sufficient information to make the real decisions." This is institutionalized narcissism, the leader's belief that only he or she can make the decisions which everyone else should support. It illustrates the belief that absolute power corrupts absolutely.

The irony of this narcissism is that very frequently it is not a problem initiated by the leader, but one which he or she has inherited. It can be a result of the condition of the institution rather than the particular style of the leader. A bishop is an excellent example. First, in most churches he is chosen for life. Secondly, admired by lay people and clergy alike, he is forced to make most decisions. Consequently, peers are hard to find, especially in mission areas, and he becomes a victim of role and circumstance. This condition, exaggerated in the role of bishop, is common to leadership at executive levels. It is particularly reinforced when the leader receives additional benefits and a much higher salary than his or her staff.

Looking at our third scale, obedience to the leader and the development of hierarchical structures within the organization naturally follow. One positive reason for hierarchy and the obedience system that goes with it is its efficiency when one has limited skilled resources, when there is an emergency, or when there is a lot of pressure for quick results. After all, when does one have the time to be democratic in such situations? Being a member of a military operation during a war is a clear example.

Hierarchy necessarily reinforces competition. If there is only one boss and I want to be president, I must compete. In the church this has become a serious problem. Since most bishops are elected for life and there is only one in most dioceses, the parish priest has limited possibilities to move upward. Since it is also less than modest to be competitive, he finds himself trapped in a vocational one-way street. When the middle line is crossed and the mature person is seized by the vision of intimacy and union, the problems of competition can be overcome. Hierarchy becomes delegation, and a new level of trust is discovered as the leader shares and listens more deeply.

In the past, obedience meant that you did as you were told for the good of the organization. Today obedience means that leader and skilled follower share and listen to each other and reach a mutual decision. Time is taken to exercise human dignity, which leads to a deeper sharing of intimacy. At the institutional level limited listening and sharing occur to bring about appropriate delegation that will humanize all concerned. The danger here is that persons who are not skilled in interpersonal relations will often confuse personal sharing and intimacy with institutional need and turn an administration into a therapy group. Disastrous consequences can result.

Delegation here means that the leader recognizes the limitations of individuals and realizes that much more can be accomplished with a team of skilled equals who work with a strong commitment to mutual and creativity accountability. At the highest level intimacy in the institutional setting is the creation of interdependent administrative communities in which total delegation is possible. Hierarchy becomes not only unnecessary but a hindrance to human dignity and personal creativity. As we shall see in the next chapter, these communities as support systems are essential to permit leadership to function at this level.

Intimacy and union are then individual rather than institutional states of growth. There is, however, an institutional connection. At this level, the institution as a system of support and delegation provides the context and the value reinforcement that encourages and permits exceptional levels of spiritual growth to occur. In fact, without this reinforcement such growth is highly unlikely. Jesus, for example, did not live in a vacuum; he spent most of his public ministry creating a support system of twelve apostles, all of whom except one became exceptional leaders in their own right.

Powers of Coercion

What is of particular significance with the three sets of forces we have reviewed is the way they connect to form coercive forces in our lives to goodness or evil. Each of us grows up in relationship to the primary institution in which we find our ministry. We are persons as systems. In the creative situation there is motion backwards and forwards between our influence on a system and its influence on us. The majority of persons feel powerless in a system and often a little afraid of what may happen if they question authority. They have good reason, for when evil is experienced at its most powerful, it is, for the most part, a system experience. Let us look at how this occurs.

The Forces of Evil

Each of us experiences in our lives a constant pull to the negative end of our scale. Although self-perservation, security, and self-centeredness are not always bad in themselves, our most destructive side is likely to emerge when they become our primary concern. When all three are our main priorities, the phenomenon of evil takes over and we become possessed. This state of possession, a system phenomenon, takes over in a systematic way; it is institutional in nature.

First, the self-preservation button is pushed. Let us imagine that you are running a small printing business. You have lost two major customers who moved to another part of the country. In order to survive you must work harder and produce more. As the pressure increases, you become more and more insecure and you feel the need for more control. You watch the books closely, take over the administration, and start setting up rules to prevent needless spending. As your anxiety increases, you become more controlling not only at the office but at home, also. Working long hours, you are not attentive to the family when you come home. As the pressure continues and your very survival seems to be at stake, feelings of tension and insecurity about the future mount. As a result, you increase management and administrative control and push your employees to produce more in less time.

The tension now produces its own momentum. Only you can make final decisions relating to new business. Only trusted employees have access to you. The business has become more of a hierarchy than before. Efficiency as well as productivity are now the exclusive values that determine whether or not a person remains with the company. The staff is less trusting and more competitive which is necessary for the company to survive. Loyalty to the company and the boss is essential. What is morally right now is to beat the competition.

Obedience to your authority as boss is uppermost. You worry to yourself, "If they do not do what I ask them right away, how on earth can I trust them with anything?" Narcissism finally begins to take over. Only the boss can make important decisions. For the person who experiences this kind of pressure, all decisions become important. You now find yourself watching not only everything, but everyone.

At this point, possession can occur, a point at which anybody's opinion is suspect that does not support one's own opinion. Such a person, completely closed off to the opinions of others, cannot be reached. At its worse, possession is reinforced by drug or alcohol dependency. To illustrate this further, let us look at the left side of our diagram again.

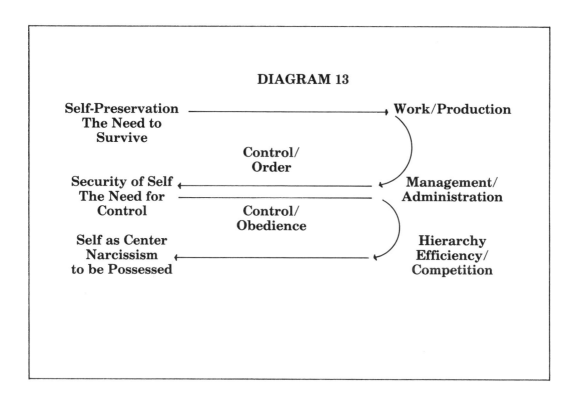

DIAGRAM 13

Self-Preservation ——————————→ Work/Production
The Need to
Survive

Control/
Order

Security of Self ←————————————— Management/
The Need for ——————————————— Administration
Control
Control/
Obedience

Self as Center ←————————————— Hierarchy
Narcissism Efficiency/
to be Possessed Competition

The diagram illustrates the movement from self-preservation through work to increased management control. The active value here is control as the person seeks to find order out of the chaos he or she experiences. As the pressure mounts, the diagram shows a movement towards a greater need for security and control, proceeding to an even more controlling system of management and administration. At this point, the active value of control becomes obedience as the person makes greater demands and becomes more hierarchical and bureaucratic. The movement is finally complete in the experience of narcissism and possession. Erich Fromm posits that this is the borderline between sanity and insanity:

A particular instance of narcissism which lies on the borderline between sanity and insanity can be found in some men who have reached an extraordinary degree of power. The Egyptian pharaohs, the Roman Caesars, the Borgias, Hitler, Stalin, Trujillo—they all show similar features. They have obtained absolute power; their word is the ultimate judgment of everything, including life and death; there seems to be no limit to their capacity to do what they want. They are gods, limited only by illness, age and death. They try to find a solution to the problem of human existence by the desperate attempt to transcend the limitation of human existence. They try to pretend that there is no limit to their lust and to their power, so they sleep with countless women, they kill numberless men, they "want the impossible." This is madness, even though it is an attempt to solve the problem of existence by pretending that one is not human. It is a madness which tends to grow in the lifetime of the afflicted person. The more he tries to be god, the more he isolates himself from the human race; this isolation makes him more frightened, everybody becomes his enemy, and in order to stand the resulting fright he has to increase his power, his ruthlessness, and his narcissism.

(*The Heart of Man*, p. 76–77)

This condition is the experience of evil we all encounter in differing degrees. It is the coercive force to the negative brought about by the peculiar combination of person and system (institution); it is the condition and experience of sin. Though neither the person nor the institution is bad in or of itself, the resultant choices that the person makes give him or her the illusion of having the power of a god, alienating him or her from the human race and God.

The examples Erich Fromm mentions above are of persons who had exceptional power, but the same experience is available to anyone who works and lives in an institution and takes their ministry seriously. Temptation comes to all of us. Consider the temptation of Jesus early in his ministry:

Full of the Holy Spirit, Jesus returned from the Jordan, and for forty days was led by the spirit up and down the wilderness and tempted by the devil. All that time he had nothing to eat, and at the end of it he was famished. The devil said to him, "If you are the Son of God, tell this stone to become bread." Jesus answered, "Scripture says, 'Man cannot live by bread alone.'" Next the devil led him up and showed him in a flash all the kingdoms of the world. "All this dominion I will give you," he said, "and the glory that goes with it; for it has been put in my hands and I can give it to anyone I choose. You only have to do homage to me and it shall be yours." Jesus answered him, "Scripture says, '"You shall do homage to the Lord your God and worship him alone.'" The devil took him to Jerusalem and set him on the parapet of the temple. "If you are the Son of God," he said, "throw yourself down; for Scripture says, 'He will give his angels orders to take care of you,' and again, 'They will support you in their arms for fear you should strike your foot against a stone.'" Jesus answered him, "It has been said, 'You are not to put the Lord your God to the test.'" So, having come to the end of all his temptations, the devil departed, biding his time.

(NEB, Luke 4: 1–13)

In this passage the devil is absolute narcissism or possession because he offers Jesus all the power he wants over man and over life itself. Jesus, of course, turns him down.

We are all open to these experiences since the seed of narcissism is within the nature of all of us. The president of a large electronics firm called me in once for consultation and asked me what the problem was with the head of accounting. "I would not know," I said. "I know very little about your company. I have not yet met the man you are speaking of." He replied that I did not need to know anything, that he (the president) would tell me. "Why do you need me?" I asked. "I need you to back me up so I can fire him," he said. As I came to know him better, I discovered that he delegated almost none of his authority and did all the hiring for the company himself, even of secretaries. This was a company of 400 employees.

In a consultation with a parish in the Eastern United States I discovered a middle-aged pastor who informed me upon arrival from some three thousand miles distant that although he had agreed with the bishop to invite me, there was nothing that could be done. "You see," he said, "this is out-and-out warfare. They are out to destroy me and my ministry." Upon further investigation I learned that he and his wife had moved there just six months before. The previous pastor, very conservative in his approach to liturgy and outreach programs, had been in charge for 25 years. The congregation, fifty percent retired people, wanted the security of tradition and personal pastoral care that the former minister had given them.

Five years before this incident, a new university was established in the area. Several of the faculty and students joined the congregation but did not feel welcome. They felt the church should be more involved in outreach to the students on campus. When the old pastor retired, some of the newcomers made sure that they were elected to the search committee for a new man.

The committee drew up a new profile and, with the approval of the bishop, began their search for a new pastor. The profile was heavily weighted towards someone who would make mission and outreach a first priority, which, the committee argued, would increase the size of the congregation and bring in more revenue. The older sector of the congregation, glad to give some newer members responsibility, appeared to agree.

The new pastor arrived and started to do his job as he saw fit. Within three months a youth club was begun and a chaplaincy initiated at the university. With the influx of students, the parish naturally had to adapt the liturgy to the spirit of the times. The new pastor did not visit the older people as had the previous rector, nor did his wife, who taught school, attend the women's group.

By the fourth month gossip had spread and the bishop received a letter stating that the pastor was not getting on well with his wife. Soon more letters arrived suggesting that he had been seen in town with another woman, and that a large percentage of the congregation wanted his resignation. The bishop called the pastor who, angry and indignant, informed the bishop that he was fifty years old and would never find another job if he left the parish. His very vocation he felt was at stake. When the bishop asked him about "this other woman," he refused to answer, replying, "I will not dignify the question by giving it an answer."

The letters continued to arrive at the bishop's office. Finally he visited the parish where at a parish-wide meeting an organized group suggested that, given the turmoil and "lack of Christian love," the pastor resign. In a fit of anger he did resign, asking to remain as pastor for six months until he found a new job.

My investigation revealed that the problem was largely due to historical circumstance. The pastor's marriage was a very good one; there was no other woman. The survey also exposed much malicious gossip involving at least ten persons, the identities of whom were unknown. The consultation ended unhappily. When a meeting was called of the parish leadership to openly discuss the events of the past in a spirit of mutual forgiveness, all parties refused. The pastor and his supporters met privately and in a public address demanded repentance of his enemies and the withdrawal of certain persons from the church. He also demanded absolute support of and fealty to his ministerial style. In response, half of the church leadership came to every parish meeting shouting for his removal from the church and continuing to accuse him of living an immoral life.

On close examination, the parish was possessed. As one listened to individual stories, they seemed reasonable and credible. Every person, however, insisted that the other side was entirely wrong and, interestingly enough, evil. Convinced that his or her ultimate values were being threatened, each parishioner was in a state of self-preservation. Many of the older people felt their church and system of security were being taken from them. The pastor felt he would never find another parish and that his view of what it meant to be a Christian was at stake. The whole situation reminded me of two armies walking toward each other in a thick fog crying, "Kill, kill," but never seeing or appreciating the other side. Tragically, each side felt it was absolutely right and both had fallen victim to the evil of narcissism. They had become possessed, and the innocent suffered. One might conclude that this could only happen in a parish or religious setting, but we know this is not true. As I looked closer, I realized that half the people involved worked at the university or were executives in local industries.

The Forces of Good

As we have already discussed, when an individual achieves a certain point of spiritual maturity, he or she is grasped by values that pull him or her forward to higher levels of development away from the power of evil. This is the experience of grace. It is a gift of possibility because the opportunity does not guarantee that a person will carry through. Narcissism, after all, does have much to offer: comfort, security, and absolute power.

What do we mean in saying that we are grasped by these values? This actually defies human explanation. The element of faith must enter in, but that we will discuss later. At this point, we can agree that to be a follower of Jesus Christ means that in human terms I seek to be energized by the same values he was energized by. James Fenhagen, in a book called *Mutual Ministry*, writes that

> To become a disciple means to see for oneself the values that energized the life of Jesus of Nazareth, to struggle with them, until there comes that moment when by the grace of God they become our own.
>
> (*Mutual Ministry: New Vitality for the Local Church*, p. 49)

To be grasped by such values is to experience the grace of God in our lives. We were created in the image of God and these values are thus an innate part of our nature just as much as our needs for self-preservation, security, and narcissism. The values that grasp us from the future are ecority and creativity, truth and meaning, and intimacy and union. Our expanded diagram now looks as follows.

The logical conclusion in looking at our diagram would be that if a person is worried about survival, the solution might lie in looking at the opposite end of the continuum, at their need for creativity and harmony. This is not the case, however. The solution to human and spiritual growth begins at the opposite end of the whole diagram at the need for intimacy.

There is, however, a connection. We mentioned earlier that family, at least historically, is an extension of the need to survive. In the family we begin to learn all of our interpersonal skills, the end point of which is the capacity for intimacy. In another publication, *The Personal Discernment Inventory*, I describe the development of interpersonal skills as

> The ability to act with generosity and understanding towards others that flows from a knowledge of oneself. It is the ability to objectify one's own feelings so that cooperation rather than isolation is enhanced.
>
> (Brian P. Hall, p. 44)

Intimacy at the human level is the sharing of one's deepest hopes, joys, anxieties, and fears with an equal who shares the same with you. Even here, however, as Thomas Oden points out, an element of personal union occurs:

> Intimates are aware that their most significant exchanges are not merely body transactions, but as persons in encounter, or the meeting of spirit with spirit. What really happens in intimacy has to do with the spirit-spirit communion or interpersonal communion, two persons experiencing their beings poignantly united. When they are most together they are most aware of that which transcends their togetherness. Their oneness reflects a deeper capacity for coherence in the universe. Their interpersonal communion echoes some abyssal capacity given in and with reality itself for communion.
>
> (*Game Free: A Guide to the Meaning of Intimacy*, p. 23)

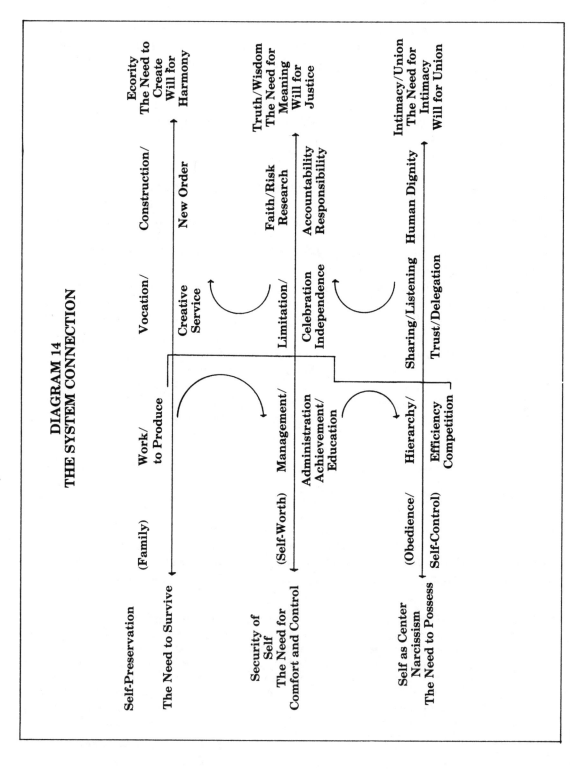

DIAGRAM 14
THE SYSTEM CONNECTION

This experience of union within the human experience of intimacy with another person includes revelations of even more significance. Evelyn Underhill, writing on the development of man's spiritual consciousness, noted that this will for union is a gift that makes man capable of union with God. As we study the lives of the mystics we discover that one obvious consequence of divine union was their increased capacity for intimacy with other human beings. The very act of intimacy is thus contemplative in nature. It demands full attention and wonder at the beauty of the pure being of the other. Contemplative prayer is no less the adoration and union with God our Father.

As we look at the intimacy scale, contemplation at the human level becomes the dignifying of the human being. It is the acting out of the value of human dignity which leads automatically to deeper concern, sharing, and listening to others. It evolves into empathetic listening. At the institutional level, with intimacy emerges the quality leader, the leader as shepherd. We must understand that contemplative listening and sharing enables us to see the values of the other and often leads to the necessity of confronting as well as affirming an individual.

As the person of the shepherd leader moves through his or her capacity for interpersonal communion to deeper levels of sharing and trusting, delegation naturally follows, exposing both follower and leader to a new awareness of freedom to be themselves. Along with the freedom comes a renewed sense of their individual limitations which causes some to withdraw. If we are able to face our shortcomings, however, laugh about them, and even celebrate them, new freedom as independence is mobilized. This is not the sort of independence that can easily regress to narcissism again because it has emerged from its opposite, intimacy.

We are experiencing the coercive force between persons and institutions that is a power to the good. Heavily reliant on the spiritual quality of the leader, it is quite different from the other side of our consciousness map where the leader was for the most part a single individual in a hierarchical structure. Here the leader must necessarily not only delegate but be a follower in a world of peers. He or she may be the functional head, bishop, or executive director, but to mobilize this force to the good, he or she must be able to delegate authority even one hundred percent at times. This is the condition of limited intimacy within the organizational sphere. It is not possible unless the leader has this personal ability to be intimate outside the work setting. This leader, both a shepherd and a lover, is a shepherd leader.

As the movement continues, the independence of others naturally introduces new knowledge as one's staff shares as equals. The main quality required here is the continued ability to risk, to have faith in the God-given potential of others. Faith at this point implies a mutual condition of accountability and responsibility.

If the contemplative listening we mentioned earlier was that and nothing else, it would remain superficial at best. The element of accountability implies a search and pursuit of the truth of a person, involving such questions as, "Do you have the skills and confidence to do the job or not?" It is the ability to confront one another creatively and move beyond the limitations to constructive strategy and planning. Implied are the leader's skills in value-oriented goal setting and concern that the institution reflect in its management structure the values that the leadership declares it will live by.

The key to understanding the movement at this point is to see that it is in essence an expansion of choices and possibilities whereas at the other end of the scale the opposite movement towards narcissism is to tighter restriction of choices. Greater interpersonal communion exposes one to others' ideas, and to become independent is the opportunity to not only choose but also act in new ways. Such opportunity is life-giving and energy-producing. It is precisely the feeling of having been loved (intimacy) and the freedom to make choices that gives the human being meaning. The discovery of meaning is actually the discovery of truth.

A concern raised at this juncture is the problem of discerning what choices and actions are necessary to maximize the growth and quality development of the institutions we live with. Discernment is a critical part of the growth and movement at this end of the scale. Again, the major difference between the movement toward intimacy and the movement toward survival is that in the latter, the person is responding to external pressures while in the former the pull is from within and demands discipline and will.

In the Christian traditions of spiritual direction, we see this movement of creatively seeking the truth in a spirit of love as guided by the Holy Spirit. The central process of spiritual guidance involves discernment of spirits, the act of prayerfully making life-giving choices which are in harmony with God's call for the individual or the system.

Finally, the movement at the second level inspired by this need for Meaning includes a passion for justice. The movement up, having been initiated in intimacy and human dignity, is now acted out institutionally as a concern for justice and the rights of all people. Until this point, however, the movement is related to the individual as shepherd leader, as he or she deals with others in an institutional setting. The upswing on our diagram continues as the pursuit of truth and the need for meaning are specified through discernment in the context of Vocation as Service.

This part of the movement is the foundation in the leader of his or her specific ministry. Having shared and examined one's limitations, having risked choices and decisions in faith and having discovered and discerned truth and meaning in a "We" context through the Spirit's guidance, I become aware of what ministry is for me. Shepherd leadership now begins to emerge. The leader is certain of his or her particular vocation and sees it as a service no matter what the job because it lies within the greater context of God's salvation plan.

It is precisely this sense of being a part of the greater whole, of being grasped by a new consciousness of the infinite order of things, that draws the shepherd leader forward. It is the experience of transcendence, which is no less than the renewed awareness of one's limitations as well as infinite possibilities. This infinite future is ecority and the will for harmony, the need in each of us to create and be co-creators.

As the person moves from limitation and independence to a new sense of leader ministry which we call vocation, he or she suddenly becomes conscious in a new way of how the parts of any system or institution relate to its whole. This system awareness is the emergence in the leader of what I have called "system skills." In *The Personal Discernment Inventory*, I describe this awareness as

> That peculiar blend of imagination, sensitivity and competence which gives rise to the capacity to see all the parts of a system of administration as it relates to the whole. It is the ability to plan and design change in that system (institutions, societies, and bodies of knowledge) so as to maximally enhance the growth of the individual parts.
>
> (Brian Hall, p. 44)

In this way, the person moves finally from ministry as service, exercising their creative vocation, to the intermediate values of construction and new order. These values are the design and development of new institutional forms, new management designs that are primarily based on value rather than production. Survival is not a personal goal but rather a concern for human and global ecology and its manifestation as a harmonious whole.

The leader at this point strives in cooperation with his or her co-workers to design their institution in such a way that the resultant management structure will be the kind of community that will enhance the maximum possible spiritual growth of each person in that community. At the same time, in an effort to enhance societal growth as well, they attempt to design the institution with the same values that are in harmony with God's plan of salvation. Thus, communal development is a process of communal discernment of spirits.

We noted earlier that it was a process of contemplation and discernment which enabled a person-leader to move from intimacy to independence, accountability, and meaning. This discernment involved a high degree of faith and risk in the pursuit of truth. In the last half of the scale, the process requires not only continued contemplation and discernment, but also the discipline of detachment. Detachment is the spiritual discipline of prayer, meditation, and time management which allows one to separate oneself from daily complexity and pressure in order to be truly present with one's task, one's companions, and ultimately, with the very source of value itself, our Lord.

At this point, the institutional strain and sudden increase of complexity in the leader's life increase ten-fold. Detachment is therefore essential to continued spiritual growth and to the very survival of the shepherd leader if he or she is to remain strong at this apex of development. The practical implications of this will be dealt with in the next chapter.

Summary

We can summarize the development of the force to good and the development of the shepherd leader by once again looking at the overall picture. We notice here that the continuum for self-preservation to ecority, creativity, and harmony is called *Hope.* The continuum from security and control (a state of unfaith) to the pursuit of truth, meaning, and justice is called *Faith,* and the continuum from narcissism to intimacy and union is *Charity* or *Love.* Diagram 15 illustrates these scales.

DIAGRAM 15

Self-Preservation		Ecority
	HOPE ──────────▶	Creativity
Survival		Harmony

Security		Truth/Wisdom
	FAITH ──────────▶	Meaning
Comfort and Control		Justice

Narcissism		Intimacy/Union
	CHARITY/LOVE ──────────▶	Intimacy
Possession		Union

There are "faith, hope and charity," said Saint Paul, but "the greatest of these is charity." In the above schema, love is the starting point of spiritual growth, always initiated in the family as the development of interpersonal communion. It is also the origin of ministry and the battle against the destructive forces of evil. The coercive force to good, illustrated in diagram 16, is now easier to understand.

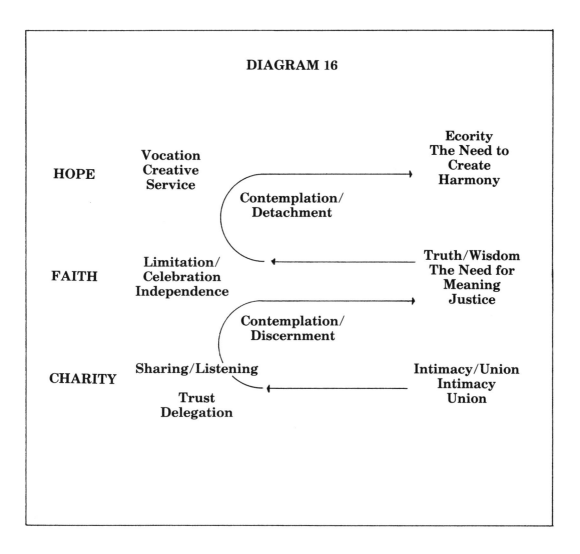

DIAGRAM 16

HOPE	Vocation Creative Service	Ecority The Need to Create Harmony
	Contemplation/ Detachment	
FAITH	Limitation/ Celebration Independence	Truth/Wisdom The Need for Meaning Justice
	Contemplation/ Discernment	
CHARITY	Sharing/Listening Trust Delegation	Intimacy/Union Intimacy Union

The movement begins with the need for intimacy and the search for union on the scale we call Charity. The motivation here is the gift of love in each of us, the first manifestation of the spirit within. This desire for love leads us to share more with others and listen attentively. We appreciate more the gifts we observe in others. The leader delegates rather than controls his or her authority. Though one is confronted with the limitation of self and others in an institutional setting, delegation creates the possibility of more independent action and thought for everyone concerned. This is the Faith scale which involves the process of contemplative discernment of choices.

Conscious of its limitations, independence, in a spirit of faith and risk, now becomes an interdependent pursuit and discovery of truth and meaning. At the level of research, interdependent minds now discover deeper knowledge.

With the exercise of mutual accountability, new levels of communal interaction give fuller meaning as greater awareness of human dignity and justice emerges. A more specific and goal-directed sense of ministry results which now emerges as leadership in the form of shepherd leadership.

The specific ministry or vocation is the call to creative service. The dimension of Hope is now pulling the shepherd to lead, which at this point calls for contemplative detachment as pressures and responsibilities increase. The vision of the leader is now global, for he or she sees the values that energized our Lord which are now calling him as not only personal but institutional. The desire for creativity now becomes the desire to be a co-creator. Ecority exceeds personal concerns for harmony in society and involves greater concerns of how to build communities and institutions so that they interface with other institutions as part of the overall plan, God's plan of history for all people.

At this last stage, an obvious irony exists. If the shepherd leader is not a great person of prayer striving to see and act through his or her daily union with the Lord, the pressures can become so strong that the demonic can once again take over. In other words, the great leader with great vision can easily conclude that the only way to do things is as he or she so directs. The leader suddenly becomes a Hitler or a Reverend Jim Jones. At every level the danger exists for evil to triumph.

The examples of the progress from intimacy to meaning and finally ecority are a little more complex in that they come at a more spiritually mature time in a person's life. The spiral downward from self-preservation to narcissism, however, can happen at any time in adult life and is therefore easier to illustrate. The following examples are therefore those of particular growth periods in the spiral upward. The first illustrates the beginning of the spiral, one common to many of us. The second assumes a fairly high level of power and maturity to begin with and deals with the second half of the upward spiral.

Examples of the Coercive to the Good

The experience of Intimacy and, to some extent, Union begins in the positive experience of family initiated by the mother caring for the child. It is the foundation for the quality experience that we have spoken of above. Many parents in finally letting go of their teenagers know what it is to sit and share with a child who has finally decided to leave home. He or she may move to get married, go to college, or even join the Peace Corps.

This experience, provided it is a positive one with understanding parents, involves intimate sharing and listening which finally lends the kind of support that encourages personal initiative and allows independence to take place. When the young person finally leaves to try things independently, everyone is a little fearful and prays it will all work out. They are aware of the movement from sharing to independence and the feelings of limitation as well as the need to have faith because of the risk involved. When the venture succeeds, new meaning and truth are learned, especially for the brave adventurer.

The first part of the movement to the good then is a natural step from a positive, reinforcing environment. This release on the part of authority, whether parents or institution, is critical to the growth of each of us. It is precisely this juncture between the person and his or her primary institution of support that characterizes growth in this sector. Through the intimacy and sharing of a creative coincidence of letting go on the part of the institutional authority and a risk taken by the individual, a leap in growth and spiritual development for the person is made possible.

Example One

As a concrete example of this, I was recently a part-time clinical director of a pastoral counseling center. There were two counselors at the center who had finished their university training as counselors in my program. As they were under my supervision, I would assign them cases and supervise those cases several hours each week which sometimes involved sitting in on the counseling sessions. Both counselors, a man and a woman in their forties, were questioning their ministries, wondering when they would be able to say with confidence that they were competent enough to run such a center on their own. Though they were both good at what they did, in my opinion they lacked experience, and particularly in the case of the woman, personal confidence.

The time came when I needed to "let go" of my work at the center and allow someone else to direct the operation. The question arose of whether we should allow the two of them to continue on their own with limited supervision or advertise for a new director. After some discernment before it was time for me to leave, I decided to let them run the operation by themselves. This meant they had to take over public relations, administration, and learn to cooperate with one another at a deeper level. With due anxiety, I removed myself from the premises so that this new relationship might take hold.

To my surprise, within three weeks, the counseling ability of each increased considerably. Not only were they cooperating, but I detected a new energy from them and a greater sense of what it means to minister. The man also began to involve himself in his own research project investigating a counseling approach more consistent with the spiritual ministry he sought. The woman seemed to grow from her new experiences in leaps and bounds.

Representing the institution, I was able to recommend at the next board meeting that they become the new co-directors of the center. Before my decision, I had spent many hours with them discussing and sharing the implications and risks involved. An intimacy condition was present from the beginning, with each person capable of sharing at profound levels. However, not until I was able to risk in faith complete delegation, to "let go," were they able to grow. As soon as the responsibility was placed upon them, the new co-directors felt more independent and, though more acutely aware of their limitations, they were able to laugh about them together. Faith and ministry were main topics of discussion and new truths about ourselves as a community evolved.

Finally, at our weekly prayer service and liturgy, they demonstrated a new sense of their vocation as pastoral counselors. They experienced greater satisfaction in being of service. Under close supervision they had not been sure of how good they were; now it did not matter so much. Their place was more clearly described and limitations were part of the faith journey.

This is just one example, the dynamics of which are no doubt common to all of us. In our journey to become shepherd leaders, we must constantly risk to allow others to grow as persons. We cannot grow unless other leaders support us and let us go. This is true of each of us no matter how powerful or limited we are because in the movement upward, leaders and followers energized by the same values are joined together in a common community of concern. In the spiral downward, hierarchy predominates and that common faith concern is irrelevant and inefficient.

In the upward spiral, a major component is the spiritual health of the leader. To let go the leader must be detached and able to trust another's capacity in a realistic way. He or she cannot do this without intimate sharing of the limitations of both parties. At this level sharing is a two way street and decisions are largely made in common.

Example Two

Father Bill, the religious leader of a community of several thousand brothers worldwide, said that be was experiencing despair at the direction his community was taking. He described his own magnificent vision for the community, one that would have global impact on world poverty. This vision required discussion and cooperation among executives of large industrial corporate interests. From his point of view, problems emerged especially at the international level when he tried to put his plan into practice. The lethargy of the brothers and the endless committee work involved, to say nothing of the travel required, produced little or no movement.

"Why do you despair?" I asked. "Because," he said, "as I travel around and experience the whole community, I realize that they only care about their immediate work. They do not really know what is going on. And when I speak to them of a community-wide plan, they tell me it has been tried before and that it will never work." "So no progress at all has been made since you have been Superior over the last five years?" I asked. "Oh yes, there has been some progress, especially in the first three years, but now everything is going too slowly. And they have so many problems that I have to listen to. In fact, I am not so sure I see the vision myself anymore."

I then asked about his ability to detach himself from the problems of others. Did he play? Did he have a close friend? Did he enjoy being at home? Looking closer at his own life, he told me that in the last three years the work day had gotten longer, that he lived in a small community with the same people he worked with, and that he had not taken a holiday in four years. Confronted by his limitations, he was sure that those he lived with would never be able to celebrate that fact. "The only thing I can do is resign," he concluded.

In Father Bill's case the upward movement had occurred but he was blocked. The institution of which he was the chief was unable to reinforce growth in him. During our discussion, however, Bill realized that not only was his own spiritual growth at stake, but also that of thousands of others in his community. His anger and exhaustion was their anger and exhaustion. Play and time to become oneself demand an attitude that begins with intimacy. Though he knew service and had at one time discovered deep meaning and truth in what he did, somewhere along the way service had become work, and work was becoming mere survival.

In the practical everyday matter of things, Bill was eventually faced with a simple series of choices: (1) To alter his living situation and live with some brothers who were peers and friends first and fellow administrators second; (2) To take some weekly play seriously; (3) To limit the hours he worked and travelled so as to enhance his own performance. He arrived at these three choices after asking himself one question: What must I do so that the quality presence I used to have with others can once again be possible?

Bill's experience is a common one for many leaders who are very lonely Shepherds. In changing his behavior, he "let go" hundreds of others in his institution. His act of release took great risk. He said at one point to me, "You can go now. Thank you for listening. I know what I have to do. The values I am really called by are obvious." Re-engaged with his original vision that had to do with the truth of his own situation, he remembered that his call was to serve, not work. God would do the work; he simply had to live a resurrection life. Ecority and harmony, by eliciting his own creativity, pulled Father Bill to be a co-creator.

In a sense, what set Bill on the road of vision and patience was a new experience of intimacy. Sometimes an outsider can help in this movement; in this particular example, I was simply a small part of God's plan for him. I have witnessed many instances similar to this where the leader decided to withdraw. It is a constant battle with no guarantees as to what the person will do. What is certain, however, is the grace of God, the connecting point to which is individual faith.

As evidenced by the above examples, the faith connection is always both personal and institutional. Jim Fenhagen, speaking of Christian community, says that if it is to be in touch with the future, "it must find ways in its own institutional life to bear witness to the simplicity of the Gospel, while at the same time giving support and encouragement to those who are trying to live simply." (*Mutual Ministry: New Vitality for the Local Church*, p. 137) The question of faith, strategies for spiritual development, and shepherd leader integration is the subject of our next chapter.

5. Living the Faith: Strategies for Integration

Introduction

This final chapter will discuss the requirements needed to sustain high levels of spiritual maturity. The focus of this work has been ministry and ministry leadership. As we have noted thus far, the leader always works within an institutional community. As each of us grows spiritually we recognize that our lives form a battlefield between the forces of good and evil. Spiritual writers of all ages have frequently asked how we can discern and choose directions that follow the good forces and confront the evil. How do we live our lives in accordance with God's plans for all of us?

The call of the shepherd lover as leader is precisely to discern the choices that will enhance the spiritual growth of all persons working in that institution and further God's plans of salvation. For the religious leader it is difficult because of the voluntary nature of the system, and for the shepherd leader ministering in a secular institution it is difficult because he or she must allow change to occur within narrow limits and goals set by the business world. Both jobs are stressful and both need extensive support if evil is to be thwarted.

To discern spirits the minister leader must be: (1) constantly developing his or her own spiritual and emotional life and (2) constantly supported and developed by his or her primary institutional community or communities.

These require the development of resources and the conscious planning of strategies for spiritual growth. These strategies, which we will call Resources, are the subject matter of this final chapter. I have divided the chapter into two parts: Framework One dealing with personal spiritual resources for Shepherd Lover development and Framework Two which discusses the communal resources necessary for Shepherd Lover development.

FRAMEWORK ONE:
Faith and the Spiritual Life

The Context. In the previous chapters we spoke of the force each of us experiences to good and to evil. A simplified diagram is pictured below.

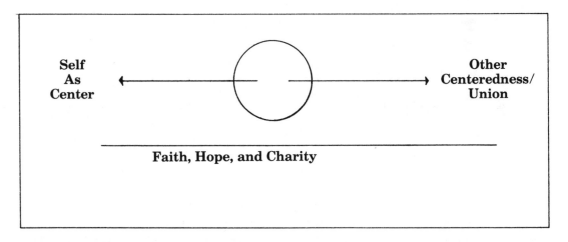

At one end are innate forces within that propel us toward self-centered satisfaction and eventually to possession, often in an institutional setting. At the other end the forces of good draw us toward other-centeredness, intimacy, truth, and union. What assurance is there that one can follow the good? At this question, an atheist must surely become a cynic. For the Christian, grace makes movement to other-centeredness possible, a movement we call our faith journey, the results of which are Hope and Charity.

Leonardo Boff writes that "grace"

> refers to the most basic and original Christian experience. It is an experience of God, whose sympathy and love for human beings runs so deep that he has given himself. It is an experience of human beings, who are capable of letting themselves be loved by God, of opening up to love and filial dialogue.
>
> (*Liberating Grace,* Orbis Books, 1979, p. 3)

Grace is thus man's and woman's most basic experience of God which implies that we believe in a God who is radically personal. The same God who created our universe, stars, galaxies, black holes, and this planet earth, who caused the creation of all biological life, made personal and direct contact with our ancestors. He created a history for us through Abraham, Moses, and the prophets, initiating through them a covenant relationship. Our natural response to this experience of God is what we call faith.

The most personal experience of God for the Christian is in the person of Jesus of Nazareth. He is therefore an experience of grace, the ultimate gift, and the embodiment of the values and priorities that God wishes us to live out in our covenantal relationship to him. Theology helps us clarify our definition of covenant as well as our understanding of Jesus as gift and what that means to us in our response of faith. Our relationship with him has given us the possibility of salvation. Just as Jesus cared for the poor and the abandoned, healed the sick, and confronted the injustices of this world, so we are called to be energized by the same values. If we agree to this, we are promised support, forgiveness when we "foul things up," and new life not only for us, but for those whom we touch. This new life, the experience of resurrection after death, gives our lives meaning, creativity, and love every time we risk for others.

As we pursue these values and are energized as Jesus of Nazareth was energized, we become one with him and move to the right of our chart rather than the left. *Right Faith is the first and most essential condition of Spiritual Growth.* It is our own personal response to our experience of God. More than an intellectual pursuit, it must be tempered by experience. As we study the Bible and the ways in which men and women of long ago experienced God, we are aware of a faith stance, a theology of what our faith is supposed to mean. Study of biblical and systematic theology, the basic tools of discernment, is therefore essential to our spiritual journey. We cannot be energized by gospel values if we do not understand the gospel. Our faith, referred to in this book as Resource One, is our most fundamental resource. Let us now examine other necessary resources for our journey.

RESOURCE TWO: Knowledge of Self

One of the central directives of spiritual leaders from every tradition is echoed in Saint Augustine's "Know thyself." Viewing this through our diagram we are preparing resources from the left side as follows:

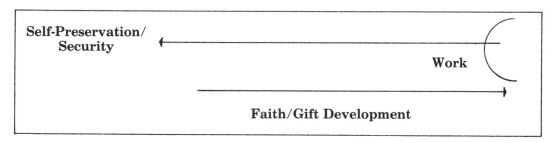

In another publication, *Leadership Through Values* (Paulist Press, 1981), I have called this resource Knowledge Integration which involves first of all basic education. To survive as a shepherd leader, each of us must be well educated and trained in our profession. We must feel competent in what we do. As Christians, we must also have a solid understanding of the sources of our faith. If I am a religious educator, I must be a competent educator and if I am an astronomer, I must be excellent in geometry and physics. Each of us as persons of faith must work hard to develop our gifts. As I grow in spiritual maturity and am called upon to lead rather than follow and perhaps become a shepherd leader as a minister, bishop, or executive in an automobile factory, there are other skills I must develop as well.

1. Pain Tolerance. Capable leaders have not only experienced great pain but have developed the capacity to make sense out of it and learn from their experiences. To experience pain without making sense of it is destructive. A young woman told her pastor, "I have been divorced. Will you allow me to teach in the adult religious education program?" He replied, "What did you learn about yourself and your faith from the experience of divorce?" Once it was clear that her faith had matured through this negative experience, the pastor realized she would be an asset as a teacher.

2. The Value of Learning. The good leader appreciates learning and realizes that we all lack knowledge some of the time. Not only the ability to learn from experience, this appreciation is also a natural curiosity for new knowledge and understanding. For example, when a person takes up a new position in another community or culture, the capable leader will always affirm the persons of that culture by extensively researching the history, needs, and unique gifts of the culture and its people.

A particularly important dimension of continuous learning is the ability to clarify the values in relation to one's faith stance. I have found that shepherd leaders, especially those working in business and industry, though often aware of their own faith are unaware of the faith stance inherent in the system they work in. Clarification of values in this instance does not lead to greater knowledge about myself as much as it does about the assumptions and presuppositions of the system that surrounds me.

In a book called *Life Maps,* Jim Fowler helped theologians view faith as a development journey: faith stances change depending on the individual level of spiritual maturity. An even greater point for the purposes of our discussion is Fowler's assertion that everyone, even the atheist, has a faith stance. Here is what we might call Fowler's triangle:

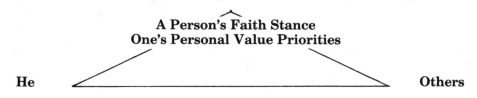

A Person's Faith Stance
One's Personal Value Priorities

He   **Others**

Fowler shows that when I talk to others, I do so through the screen of my faith and value stance. I also interpret what the "OTHER" person says through the same screen. For example, if I base my faith on the stance of self-preservation and "looking after number one," an attitude reinforced by my company which says, "Don't trust the competition or even the customer," then my stance toward others is going to be guarded at best. My distrust and disdain of competitors will prevent me from learning from them. However, if my faith stance is Christian and I believe in viewing all human beings as children of God, my attitude will be very different and I will listen to people no matter who they are. I will see them through different eyes.

Understanding and analyzing the faith stances of systems we work in is a very important learning task for the growing shepherd. Many books are valuable resources in this area, particularly Edward Stevens' *Business Ethics,* published by Paulist Press. Other resources include *Realms of Meaning* by Philip Phenix, *Deschooling Society,* and *Towards a History of Needs* by Ivan Illich, and finally *A Guide for the Perplexed* by E.F. Schumacher.

3. Administrative Skills. The capable leader must have skills in what we might call "minimal non-dependency capability." This includes not only the ability to write a good letter, but minimal facility in budgeting and flow charting of money, operating a computer terminal, and in using a typewriter.

4. Interpersonal and Group Development Skills. A leader must know how to get along with, support, and lovingly confront persons he or she works and plays with. This ability extends beyond simple one-to-one relationships to knowledge of group dynamics and community building. Without this skill, shepherd leaders are not able to build the necessary support systems they need for growth.

RESOURCE THREE:
Beyond Self-Contemplating Others

This resource is simply the recognition of the value of others as the most important resource. It is based on the presupposition that the most significant behavior for the Christian is love, the infinite respect for the value of others. This is grace in action, for I cannot love others beyond the extent to which I recognize my own infinite value. This is an implicit truth because God loved me first and completely.

This recognition is always initiated in the family which illustrates its importance and centrality. The entire field of human relations training helps develop this resource which involves four processes:

1. Contemplation, the act of being with another person with complete and total attention. It requires active listening without judgment, allowing one to see the beauty and uniqueness of the other person regardless of their negative qualities.

2. Generation is the result of contemplation. As I see another's values, gifts, and creative options, my own horizons are expanded and my options increased.

3. Reflection is the ability during the silence of listening to another to step back, help the other clarify, and reflect on his or her own values, gifts, and options. It is the prelude to choice and action.

4. Action or Construction is the final result of the process. Having seen and loved another, it is hoped that the other person is moved to responsible action in the world. The contemplator is also changed in the process. On our original diagram this resource would have been illustrated as follows:

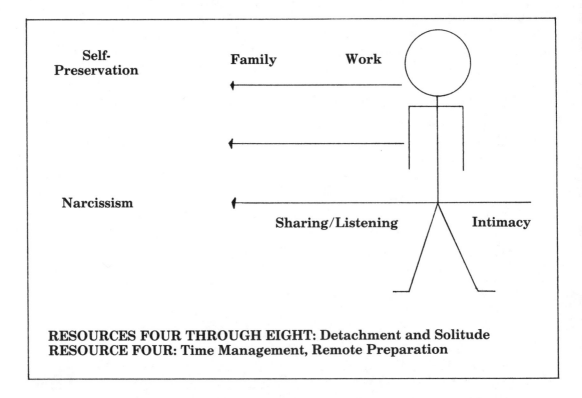

RESOURCES FOUR THROUGH EIGHT: Detachment and Solitude
RESOURCE FOUR: Time Management, Remote Preparation

Detachment is the point of separation for anyone on a spiritual pilgrimage. We separate ourselves from the pressures of the world in order to see ourselves clearly in relationship to God. It is the first and most important step in discernment for by objectively seeing ourselves this way we are then able to discern more clearly. I detach myself from the clutter in my life. The first step in such a process is time management.

What is involved here is not only the strict management of time but the struggle to harmonize work and play in my life. It is the first and most basic behavioral quality for spiritual development and survival of shepherd lovers. We are dealing with the right side of our diagram.

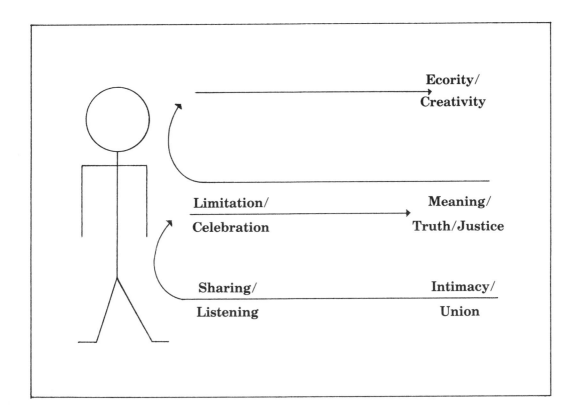

In a monumental book called *The Shape of the Liturgy,* Dom Gregory Dix wrote of how the early church and the church of the medieval period wisely adapted a process of sanctification of time. By initiating each part of the day with an office (official prayers) of praise, the day was ordered into four parts, thus sanctifying time. At daybreak the office of Lauds (Praise) would begin and the bells would toll the start of the work day. To mark the sixth hour, at noon the office of Sext would be said. Finally Vespers, or Evensong in Old English, would be said as the light of day faded and evening approached. For the great monasteries and cathedrals of Europe, this ordering of time with parish bells and songs of praise was an attempt to build the kingdom of God on earth. More than anything else, it gave persons hope and a sense of meaning amid the squalor and disease, detaching them from the anxieties of the day.

Because the swing shift and seven-day work week today make this simple medieval formula impractical, I have suggested another approach to the ordering and sanctification of time. I first wrote about this in *Value Clarification as Learning Process: A Handbook for Religious Educators* (Paulist Press, 1973). My modern plan divides the day into our activities of Work, Maintenance, Play and Freesence.

IF SYSTEM: MEANING MAKING—FOUR ENVIRONMENTS

VALUE	DEFINITION	TIME AND PLACE	ACTIVITY	BASIC RELATIONSHIPS/ PERCEPTION
W O R K	Modification of the environment for the creative enhancement of man	Limited time specific locale, goals and ends	Doing Producing Coping	The basic people will be co-workers Institutional representatives with whom I work. Stress on duty, obligation and expectations.
M A I N T E N A N C E	Recuperation from work, care and maintenance of physical and emotional well being of self and others.	Limited in time specific to the individual or relationships maintenance.	Resting Recuperating Maintaining	Heavy emphasis on the body and self. Stress on maintenance of others for specific ends and goals of the relationships. Examples: Family Communication, Management Relations
P L A Y	Placing perspective on the world by imagining, designing and acting alternatives, stress on juxtaposition to work, excess and festivity.	Planned in-utile time, locale is chosen interdependently	Fantasizing Acting Searching Celebrating	The relationships are outside duty and obligation or expectation external to the person or group. It is always with the person I am, or might have intimate interaction with.
F R E E S E N C E	A 'being with' and contemplation of the environment. Being myself such that others present want to be themselves also.	Time and place are un-limited. Time is eternal, locale is experience of at-one-ness	Being Waiting Seeing	The relationship whether in solitude or with another person is characterized by intimacy and its consequent unifying effect.

In short, work is my basic vocation, what I do to make a living. Maintenance is what I do to maintain my body such as sleep and hygiene. Since we are social beings, however, maintenance is much more the activity of listening to and helping other people with their problems. Work and maintenance are different in that work is just there while maintenance drains energy from us. Play is the opposite of work because it is not a duty-related activity. Freesence is high play that requires the same discipline and skills as my work but like play it is re-creative for me. The difference between work and maintenance on the one hand and play and freesence on the other is the human relationships involved. Consider the following diagram.

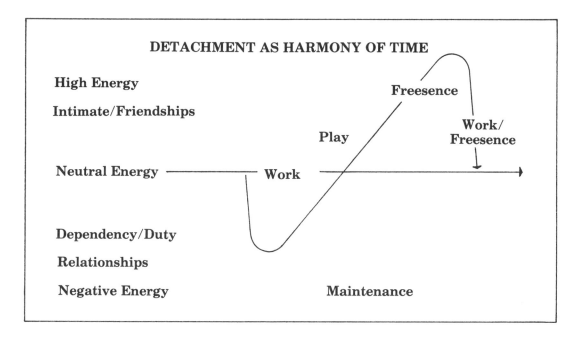

DETACHMENT AS HARMONY OF TIME

High Energy

Intimate/Friendships

Freesence

Work/
Freesence

Play

Neutral Energy ——————————— Work

Dependency/Duty

Relationships

Negative Energy   Maintenance

As illustrated, the work and maintenance sector limits the possibilities for one's relationships and tends to be energy draining. One is always bound by duty in some way to the demands of work. Work is also the basis of one's security and therefore cannot be intimate in nature. If the work involves people as most leadership positions do especially in pastoral work, then it demands much maintenance of others and drains energy.

As we move beyond maintenance and begin to relax, play is initiated, the first stage of detachment from work. When we are fully relaxed, freesence or total detachment takes over. Because the play-freesence sector requires that one be totally oneself, the relationships here are only with our most trusted intimates and friends, usually not persons I work with. When work and freesence become mixed as is often the case with enthusiastic persons in ministry, maintenance increases considerably.

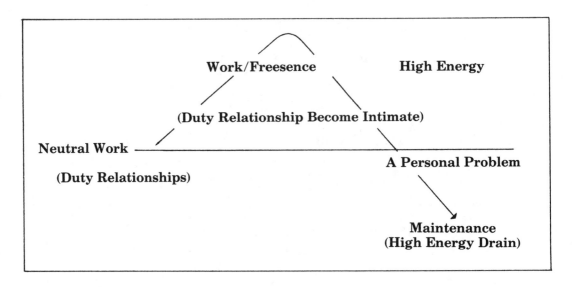

Work/Freesence   High Energy

(Duty Relationship Become Intimate)

Neutral Work ——————————————————————————

(Duty Relationships)   A Personal Problem

Maintenance
(High Energy Drain)

When we enjoy our work, we tend to work long hours and are more likely to encounter problems with intimate co-workers which cause extra drainage because of the close relationships. To grow spiritually, each of us must harmonize our use of time in all four areas. Am I working too many hours each week? Does my family see enough of me? Do I set aside time for quality play? These are the kinds of questions one must ask before detachment is achieved. Contemplative prayer emerges during play, not work. The spiritual journey demands that this balance be struck.

I have found the following four Discernment Questions helpful in aiding persons who are seeking this balance in order to be detached:

Question One: Work. What is the most you can do before you compromise the highest quality which is you? You should answer this question by giving a specific number of hours. What is the most you can do before you compromise the highest qualities of those around you whether family or co-workers?

Question Two: Work/Play Ratio. What minimal recreation do you need to forget the worries of work? This should be answered with a specific time schedule for each week. What are you doing to develop play and freesence activities?

Question Three: Maintenance. What amount of listening and what range of activities can you accept before the best you can be is compromised? This should be answered with respect to time limits on activities that are most draining such as counseling.

Question Four: Maintenance/Play Ratio. What minimal support do you need from friends and those with whom you work in order to be the best person you can be?

RESOURCE FIVE:
The Body

Jesus began his ministry by fasting for forty days alone in the desert. Though he probably drank a little water he ate nothing for the entire period. His physical condition must have been excellent for him to fast for such a long time. Following his example, the first rule of detachment and preparation for prayer after time management is to take care that we are in optimum physical health. For the shepherd lover this means that he or she pays serious attention to his or her own health. Care must be taken to avoid excessive alcohol, cigarettes, and the use of any chemicals for emotional support. Attention must be given to: (1) Daily diet, weight, and blood pressure; (2) Regular physical exercise; (3) Consideration of fasting when one's physical condition allows. When one looks and feels in good physical shape, personal sense of worth improves and one's presence among others is enhanced. If we are anxious about worries and problems, physical exercise can dissipate our excess energy. Books on this topic are plentiful. Three to begin with are: *The Royal Canadian Air Force Exercise Plans for Physical Fitness*, *The New Aerobics* by Kenneth Cooper, and *Diet for a Small Planet* by Frances Moore Lappe.

Finally, an important aspect of this concern for the body is fasting. As we have noted, however, it must not be done without overall attention to the body through diet and exercise. As it was for Christ, fasting has always been a central part of the spiritual discipline of persons throughout the ages. Fasting is total abstinence from food for at least two and a half days with constant drinking of water. It can be extended for as long as forty days but this takes great care and planning. Its benefits are numerous, especially in the development of the quality of meditation and contemplative detachment. For those who pursue this discipline a few reminders might be helpful: (1) Fasting must be embarked on only after sufficient preparation through diet and exercise; (2) Check with a medical doctor to insure that your health is good enough to carry out such a venture; (3) Fasting should never be done alone but rather as a community experience; (4) After an extended fast, gradual assimilation of liquids is necessary for several days before solid foods can be eaten; (5) The length of the fast must be agreed to before it begins. It must be ended at this time and not extended by individuals who want to lose weight or do not feel hungry. Some books I would recommend are Louis Fischer's *The Life of Ghandi* and *Fasting Rediscovered, A Guide to Health and Wholeness for Your Body Spirit,* by Thomas Ryan.

RESOURCE SIX:
Scripture and the Office

For the Christian, the values and priorities we live by are the values that energize us in life-giving ways. We make contact with such values by beginning our daily prayer and meditation with the reading of Scripture and the psalms, the record of others in history who tried to live out those same values through their contact with the Lord of History. Although study of the Bible is important to understand the faith, the pure experience of it through daily reading is equally important. Daily reading should be regular and steady throughout the year and in harmony with the seasons of the church. There are a number of different creative lectionaries, daily bible and psalms appropriate for this purpose. In the past, this sequencing has been provided by the monastic breviary or daily office read in the morning and evening by the clergy and religious communities. Its value is not nearly so narrow; it is an essential form of prayer for all serious Christians who have a ministry.

There are many resources available. One possibility is to read from a version of the Bible which most strongly helps you experience what you are reading about. Annotated versions of the Bible are helpful in this regard. Some I have found especially helpful are the *Jerusalem Bible, The New American Bible, The Good News for Modern Man,* and the *New English Bible.* Current office books may also be used. An excellent one is the *Prayer Book Office* compiled by Howard Galley and published by Seabury Press. Another is the *Monastic Breviary* developed by the Order of Holy Cross. An interesting ecumenical office, *The Daily Office,* is published by S.P.C.K., London, England.

Daily reading is not only an intellectual pursuit but also an experience of the death-resurrection cycle. The psalms, the Old and New Testaments, and especially the Gospels are a constant reliving of the cycle of life, death, and resurrection. When read, they connect with the archetypes in each of us, aiding our personal spiritual journeys. The last three resources, Time Management, the Body, and the reading of Scripture are traditionally referred to as Remote Preparation. The next three are the ingredients necessary for Meditation.

RESOURCE SEVEN:
Relaxation

When we relax we reduce the anxiety and tension in the body and mind. As this happens we become more present to the moment and to those around us. Anxiety is worry about the future which is conditioned by the past as the following diagram illustrates.

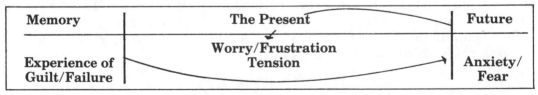

Memory	The Present	Future
	Worry/Frustration Tension	
Experience of Guilt/Failure		Anxiety/ Fear

We see that past memories of failure or guilt accumulate into the future and are experienced as anxiety or fear. These memories circle into the present and are experienced as daily tension and frustration. For example, if I forgot an appointment this morning, I may feel guilty about not remembering. I will then grow anxious about the outcome and the anger of the person I let down. This in turn makes me tense now. When I relax, the present and past disappear and with them the tension. Relaxation and non-attachment exercises (Resource Eight) help us forget and detach ourselves from these daily tensions.

The first step in relaxing for meditation is proper body posture. Any posture will do as long as the spine is straight and erect as in a sitting or kneeling position. A common posture in the East is the lotus position. The purpose is to relax and heighten attention so that we become so present to the moment and detached from worry that we become aware of the presence of God. After assuming an appropriate posture, the relaxation exercises begin. There are many standard methods involving tightening and relaxing the muscles, breathing exercises, and imagining various parts of the body and concentrating on relaxation response sentences.

For persons who have difficulty relaxing, current biofeedback training would be helpful. Two references are *Stress and the Art of Biofeedback* by Barbara Brown and *Autogenic Methods* by Schultz and Luthe (see Appendix). A very helpful volume for both body posture and relaxation for meditation is *Meditation in Depth* by Klemens Tilmann published by Paulist Press.

RESOURCE EIGHT:
Non-Attachment

These exercises, which are an extension of relaxation methods enable the person to detach him or herself from specific habits or concerns that may be troubling. This approach is the basis for most Eastern methods of meditation. A helpful text on this subject is *The Way of Non-Attachment* by Dhiravamsa published by Turnstone Press of London.

Though there are many methods of relaxation, the intention is always the same: one-centeredness and deep concentration and attention to the present. A western psychologist and the founder of Psychosynthesis, Roberto Assagioli, developed this to a fine art. For the professional spiritual director, his work *Psychosynthesis: A Manual of Principles and Techniques* published by Hobbs, Dorman and Company, is highly recommended.

A popular non-attachment method of relaxation is the mantra. An extensive work on meditation is *The Open Way: A Meditation Handbook* by Gerald May. Finally, the entire science of non-attachment in simple and helpful language can be found in a book called *Living Simply Through the Day: Spiritual Survival in a Complex Age* by Tilden Edwards. Both of these books are published by Paulist Press.

RESOURCE NINE:
Meditation

Meditation is but the period of waiting that follows Scripture reading, relaxation, and detachment, the waiting in silence for God to speak. There are various approaches to this time of waiting, one of which involves passive concentration keeping the mind blank through non-attachment processes. Other methods use images and imaging which take the mind on patterned inner journeys, a method pioneered by Roberto Assagioli. Two references that deal extensively with the inner reality image approach are *The Kingdom Within* by John Sanford and *The Other Side of Silence* by Morton Kelsey. Both works use the image approach and add the dimension of dream interpretation as a source of inner wisdom.

All of the resources mentioned thus far have stressed the preparation of the Shepherd Lover for the spiritual battle which we have called Framework One. This set of resources, however, is not sufficient on its own. To proceed successfully on the right side of the diagram, one must also have support from three other groups. This last connection is difficult because the following resources must be encouraged and in some cases are provided totally by institutions.

FRAMEWORK TWO:
The Spirit and Communal Life: The Body of Christ:
The Communal Connection

Just as it is necessary for an individual to have the right faith orientation, so the leader, particularly the shepherd lover, must have a right institutional faith, what Saint Paul called an understanding of the Body of Christ:

> Just as each of our bodies has separate parts and each part has a separate function, so all of us, in union with Christ, form one body, and as parts of it we belong to each other. Our gifts differ according to the grace given us. If your gift is prophecy, then use it as your faith suggests; if administration, then use it for administration; if teaching, then use it for teaching. Let the preachers deliver sermons, the almsgivers give freely, the officials be diligent, and those who do works of mercy do them cheerfully.
>
> (Jerusalem Bible. Romans 12: 4–8)

For Paul, the Spirit of Christ in each person forms an invisible mystical network that unites us in a cohesive organism he calls the Body. Each of us forms an interdependent whole with each other. Leaders cannot function without followers; both need each other. Each person's gifts and ministry are indispensable to the whole. Paul saw the person as a part of a system. Though individual spiritual development is important, Gerald May points out in his book *Pilgrimage Home* that

> There are some aspects of spiritual growth which require totally private self-confrontation, and there are some aspects which are so numinous that they cannot be communicated. Both of these factors make aloneness a very real and legitimate dimension of the spiritual search. Yet at the same time, there is real help from other human beings. The support of others, their critique,

guidance, and their historical heritage are not always available in one form or another, but they are absolutely necessary.

He then adds, "When we look at the panorama of human spiritual searching, three basic dimensions of aloneness and togetherness seem to emerge: the solitary journey, the dyadic, and the community." (Paulist Press, 1979, pp. 27–28)

In our diagram the final set of resources on the right side are as follows:

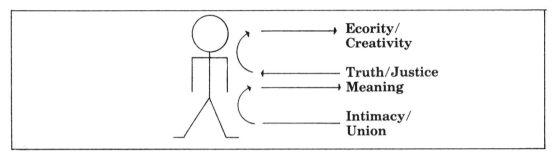

We noted in the previous chapter that the upswing caused by the coercive force to the good, the phenomenon we call grace, is a system experience, the ultimate life-giving experience. In the life of prayer it is symbolized by the community praying and breaking bread together through the Eucharist. Christ said that "when two or three are gathered together in my name, there I will be among you."

In the weekly Eucharist persons come together, each with a separate spiritual struggle, and affirm in the breaking of the bread and the sharing of the cup of wine that we are one in the Lord together. We may not feel one in the Lord or resurrected, but we are in fact a community of support. This reality stated weekly is an assertion of what is needed to remain at the right side of the diagram without being compromised. This is particularly true of Shepherd Lovers with significant power such as bishops and other executives who are under pressure. To sustain high levels of leadership and spiritual integrity under such pressure, each person needs three additional sources of support from the system: (1) An intimacy system; (2) A work delegation and support system, and (3) a peer support system. From my own observations, when more than one of these sources is absent, the stress for a leader with considerable responsibility is very high. The less pressure from the system, the fewer supports required. To view this more clearly, let us first examine each resource separately.

RESOURCE TEN:
The Intimacy System

Persons in leadership positions and anyone who wishes to grow spiritually must share intimately with at least one other person on a regular basis. In an intimate relationship, there need not be a sexual dimension, but simply an experience of deep sharing. Intimacy implies regular sharing of all my fears and hopes openly with another person who shares equally with me. It is not counseling or spiritual direction as much as sharing with a peer. Why is such a relationship necessary?

As each of us grows in spiritual maturity and becomes more extroverted in our service to others, we need to see ourselves as others see us, perhaps the most important step in reaching maturity. Part of growing spiritually is the ability to integrate our inner perceptions of ourselves with the impressions we give to others. Only deep and honest sharing allows others to see us clearly. This kind of sharing, which is called dyadic, is not possible without regularity. Though the most natural setting for such sharing is the marriage relationship, marriage is no guarantee of intimacy. Intimacy requires nurturance between two persons over a long period of time; it is growth in mutual trust and radical commitment to loyalty and confidentiality.

Since intimacy is a need each of us has and also a requirement for spiritual growth, it presents a problem for many persons in leadership positions. For the celibate priest or sister, intimacy is too often marred by concerns about homosexuality or physical involvement. Of course, risks are involved, but a much wider view of human relationships is at stake. Persons in leadership positions with weak marriages have the same legitimate fears. These concerns reflect other problems which must be cared for. Whatever the extenuating circumstances, intimate sharing is essential for exceptional growth.

The intimate relationship as a spiritual necessity cannot be with a co-worker. A true play relationship, by its very nature is free from the pressure to produce. Intimacy is a gift available to anyone regardless of their vocation. Finally, it often will not occur unless the institution I live in, family or community, encourages it and sees it as valuable. For example, many religious congregations I have worked with discouraged any close relationships in or out of the system. It is not unusual to find a superior general of a community of either men or women isolated and lonely because of his or her authority, yet unable to consult with other superiors outside the congregation, especially of the opposite sex. "Why?" I ask. "Because it is simply frowned upon," is the reply. "We are supposed to be self-sufficient."

Intimacy therefore needs to be encouraged by our institutions, but only in open and healthy ways. In a celibate context, for example, it can be encouraged only after a system-wide exploration and discussion of what healthy interpersonal relationships are and their limits. How to form such relationships is beyond the scope of this book. We can say, though, that it requires minimal maturity and skill ability. Intimacy is a sign of higher levels of spiritual and leadership functions. For many, it may be only a discernment question. Is it essential to spiritual growth in my institution? Is it discouraged and if so, what are the implications of the discouragement and what can be done about it? Do I share intimately with another person in my own life?

RESOURCE ELEVEN:
Work Delegation and Support

Unlike the intimacy system, this resource involves the development of a support community with the persons I work with. There are two prerequisites for such a community: (1) Anything I do can, if necessary, be delegated for a limited period of time, and (2) The team I am part of supports me and each other. The work team should whenever possible be a team of peers.

The first condition alludes to the fact that such a community cannot exist without support from the institution. For me to delegate all I do, the persons I work with must have just as many skills and as much authority as I have. An individual may not have this, but a team will. Without delegation, total detachment from work, even when the leader is tired and exhausted is not possible.

The second prerequisite states the necessity for a support community of peers to allow optimum working conditions. I define peers as chosen equals who are more skilled and competent in certain areas than I am, and to whom I am willing to delegate my authority. The problems of shepherd leadership become apparent at this point. These conditions obviously cannot come about through either the enthusiasm of the leader or institutional reinforcement. Both leader and institution must work in harmony. The institution provides the financial and spiritual resources and the leader must be mature enough to risk delegation for a higher vision.

Here are some common problems. A bishop of a new diocese has no staff and minimal budget, enough only for a secretary and a part-time helper. How can he put together a work team? To whom can he delegate? He cannot do either until the system provides funds or voluntary help. If he receives either, it will still take months of community building before he can delegate any authority.

Often a person will hold an executive position with every financial resource at his or her disposal, but the wrong system reinforcements. A common example is the executive with a staff of five co-workers. All are professionals with equal skills but unequal salaries. It is very common in a church to find the chief pastor earning twice the salary of everyone on the staff. A woman professional is frequently paid less than the man. These are but a few examples of the institutional reinforcements that make spiritual growth beyond a certain point impossible.

Collegial leadership is essential for individual and institutional growth beyond a certain point. It involves not only a constant struggle against bigotry and fear of losing one's authority but also training new people, firing others, examining personal limitations, and risking institutional disapproval. This work delegation and support system does not come naturally, but must be planned. The leader must initiate it and then later it becomes criteria for good leadership in a system and is encouraged as a positive force for spiritual growth.

RESOURCE TWELVE:
Peer Support System

The peer support system is a group of persons at my professional level who are not a part of my system but with whom I meet regularly to share ideas and receive feedback. These groups are common at professional society meetings, seminars, and annual conferences. Bishops meet other bishops and engineers meet other engineers. Though executives need to meet other executives at the same professional level, they need not be from the same discipline. Bishops should meet Superior Generals, bankers, and scientists. These meetings are best in small groups of less than fifteen persons which get together regularly several times a year to share in a structured setting. In his discussion of peer consultation in pairs, Caplan says:

> Peer consultation is a process of borrowing and lending. From this process of interchange of ideas, abilities, knowledge, conceptualizing skills and workable schemes comes a mutual enrichment which enables both parties to face their respective tasks with increased enthusiasm.
> (*Support Systems and Mutual Help,* edited by G. Caplan and M. Killilea, Grune and Stratton, New York, p. 270)

The persons involved are neither one's intimate friends nor co-workers, but a different person or group of persons from whom I can receive wise feedback about work or play relationships without threat. The role of a spiritual director has been seen as an authority figure, spiritual maturity changes the director's view. Therefore at the level of leadership discussed here, peer consultation is one form of spiritual direction.

Though most institutions support professional development, few provide financial assistance for the necessary consistent support. An exception is the bishop-to-bishop peer consultation provided through the Office of Pastoral Development of the Episcopal church in the United States. When a bishop is elected and consecrated, he is asked to pair with a bishop from across the country. The church provides financial assistance for the program and the bishops are trained in structured consultation. The training insures that they relate as wise peers, not as counselors or problem solvers. This is but one example of how such peer support can only come with system reinforcement.

Conclusions

In this book I have tried to raise questions as well as suggest some solutions, but for many of the questions there may be no answers. The issue for me is not to provide answers, but how to make fewer mistakes. In this last chapter, I have suggested a list of twelve resources for personal and spiritual growth. Attention to these resources, however, does not guarantee the spiritual development of the leader. Spiritual development is a gift that requires more than the effort any of us can produce. Why then are these resources listed?

They are simply a list of minimum requirements for the possibility of spiritual growth at certain levels of leadership maturity. Though many more could be added, these will help us make fewer mistakes in our journeys through life as sons and daughters of God.

One misunderstanding presented by this book might be that the battle is over once we have achieved spiritual maturity and embraced the grace that makes union with our Lord possible. Unfortunately, it is not this easy. Life is a struggle between good and evil up to the last moment. That struggle is within ourselves, our leaders, and our institutions. It is hard work all the way. There are effective and ineffective ways of mobilizing the energy and support we all need to grow. This book is intended as an aid in understanding the process of celebrating our limitations and trying to make fewer mistakes.

Finally, the support groupings and relationships suggested in this last chapter are not definitive by any means. We have our friends, our solitude, our co-workers, those we trust as peer consultants, and if we are lucky, someone we are intimate with. Some might even be intimate with our Lord. As we age and mature, we discover the need not to confuse these groupings which can limit certain kinds of growth. To be intimate with my secretary can cause problems; to delegate secretarial work to my wife can lead to trouble; to play only with those at work and not my family is unwise. These are not hard-line rules that must be followed, but simply guidelines for the possibility, not the certainty, of growth. They are meant to aid not all Christians at every level of development, but those who aspire to the level of Shepherd Lover.

A final resource must be added, one that was part of the life style of all the great saints of history. It is the ability to relate consistently to the "grass roots" and remain in constant touch with one's constituency. This is not so much a support group as a representative group. As I grow spiritually in an integrated way, my ability to communicate personally with the grass roots of my system also grows. Like everything else, this takes time and practice. The higher one advances in a system, the more difficult this communication becomes. One institutional approach is to insist always on certain kinds of representation on boards and at key planning events.

The whole reality comes together for me when I think of the life of the great saints and mystics. Evelyn Underhill noted that the great mystics like our Lord possessed three characteristics that were always present. First, they had a great capacity for solitude; they knew and experienced the person of Christ in their lives. He was as intimate with them as a spouse or close friend would be to anyone else. Second, they had a tremendous capacity for intimacy not only with God, but with every human being. Third, their lives had a social, sometimes global effect on every strata of society from the grass roots to Kings, Queens, Shepherds, and lovers everywhere.

Bibliography

Assagioli, Roberto M.D. *The Act of the Will*. Penguin Books, New York, 1974.

———. *Psychosynthesis: A Manual of Principles and Techniques*. Hobbs, Dorman and Company, Inc. New York, 1965.

Baillie, John. *A Diary of Reading*. Abingdon, Nashville, Tenn., 1955.

Boff, Leonardo. *Liberating Grace*. Orbis Books, New York, 1979.

Bonaventure. *The Soul's Journey into God, The Tree of Life, The Life of St. Francis*, translated by Ewert Cousins. Paulist Press, New York, 1978.

Brown, Barbara B. *Stress and the Art of Biofeedback*. Bantam Books, New York, 1977.

Caplan, G. and M. Killilea, editors. *Support Systems and Mutual Help*. Grune and Straton, New York, 1972.

Caplan, Ruth B. *Helping the Helpers to Help: Mental Health consultation to aid clergymen in pastoral work*. Seabury Press, New York, 1972.

Clark, Walter Houston, *The Psychology of Religion*. The Macmillan Company, New York, 1958.

Cooper, Kenneth H. *The New Aerobics*. Bantam Books, New York, 1970.

Dhiravamsa. *The Way of Non-Attachment*. (the practice of insight meditation) Turnstone Books, London, 1975.

Dix, Dom Gregory. *The Shape of the Liturgy*. Dacre Press, London, 1945.

Edwards, Tilden. *Living Simply Through the Day*. (spiritual survival in a complex age) Paulist Press, New York, 1977.

Erikson, Erik H. "Identity and the Life Cycle", Psychological Issues, 1,1 (1959).

Fenhagen, James C. *Mutual Ministry: New Vitality for the Local Church*. The Seabury Press, 1977.

Fischer, Louis. *The Life of Mahatma Gandhi*. Harper and Brothers, New York, 1950.

Fowler, Jim and Sam Keen. (Jerome Berryman, editor). *Life Maps: Conversations on the Journey of Faith*. Word Books, Wasco, Texas, 1978.

Frankl, Viktor E. *Man's Search for Meaning*. Washington Square Press, Inc., New York, 1963.

Fromm, Erich. *The Heart of Man*. Perennial Library, New York, 1964.

Galley, Howard, compiler and editor. *The Prayer Book Office*. Seabury Press, 1980.

Greenleaf, Robert K. *Servant Leadership*. (A journey into the nature of legitimate power and greatness). Paulist Press, New York, 1977.

Ibn 'Ata'illah. *The Bezels of Wisdom*. Translated by R. W. J. Austin, Paulist Press, New York, 1980.

Illich, Ivan. Edited by Nanda Anshen. *Deschooling Society*. Harper and Row, Publishers, New York, 1970.

———. *Toward a History of Needs*. Pantheon Books, New York, 1978.

Inge, W. R. *Personal Religion and the Life of Devotion*. Longmans Green and Company, Ltd. London, 1924.

James, William. *The Varieties of Religious Experience*. Collier Books, New York, 1961.

Jasper, Ronald C. D. *The Daily Office*. (by the Joint Liturgical Group) S.P.C.K. and the Epworth Press, London, England, 1968.

Jaynes, Julian. *The Origin of Consciousness in the Breakdown of the Bicameral Mind*. Houghton Mifflin Company, Boston, 1976.

Kelsey, Morton T. *The Other Side of Silence: A Guide to Christian Meditation*. Paulist Press, New York, 1976.

Kimper, Frank. "Self and Therapy". (unpublished) 1968.

May, Gerald G. *Pilgrimage Home*. (the conduct of contemplative practice in groups) Paulist Press, 1979.

———. *The Open Way: A Meditation Handbook*. Paulist Press, New York, 1977.

Oden, Thomas C. *Game Free: A Guide to the Meaning of Intimacy*. Harper and Row, Publishers, New York, 1974.

(Order Holy Cross) *A Monastic Breviary*. Holy Cross Publications, West Park, New York 1976.

Phenix, Philip H. *Realms of Meaning*. McGraw Hill, New York, 1964.

Rogers, Carl R. and William Coulson, editors. *Freedom to Learn*. Charles E. Merrill Publishing Company, Columbus, Ohio, 1969.

The Royal Canadian Air Force Exercise Plans for Physical Fitness. Pocket Books, New York, 1972.

Ryan, Thomas CSP. *Fasting Rediscovered. A Guide to Health and Wholeness*. Paulist Press, New York, 1981.

Sanford, John A. *The Kingdom Within*. Paulist Press, Ramsey, 1970.

Schultz, J. H. M. D. and W. Luthe, M.D. *Autogenic Methods, Volume I* edited by Wolfgang Luthe. Grune and Stratton, New York and London, Volume I: 1969.

Schumacher, E. F. *A Guide for the Perplexed*. Harper and Row, Publishers, New York, 1977.

Schweitzer, Albert, *Memories of Childhood and Youth*. Macmillan, New York, 1925.

Stern, Aaron. *Me: The Narcissistic American*. Balline Books, New York, 1979.

Stevens, Edward. *Business Ethics*. Paulist Press, New York, 1979.

Tilmann, Klemens. *Meditation in Depth*. (A practical guide to meditation for groups and individuals) Paulist Press, New York, 1979.

Underhill, Evelyn. *Mysticism: A Study in the Nature and Development of Man's Spiritual Consciousness*. Meridian Books, Cleveland, Ohio, 1955.